AFFIRMATIVE ACTION FOR THE FUTURE

AFFIRMATIVE ACTION
FOR THE FUTURE

James P. Sterba

CORNELL UNIVERSITY PRESS
ITHACA AND LONDON

Publication of this book was made possible in part by support from the Institute for Scholarship in the Liberal Arts, College of Arts and Letters, University of Notre Dame.

First published 2009 by Cornell University Press
First printing, Cornell Paperbacks, 2009
Printed in the United States of America

Library of Congress Cataloging-in-Publication Data

Sterba, James P.
  Affirmative action for the future / James P. Sterba.
    p. cm.
  Includes bibliographical references and index.
  ISBN 978-0-8014-4607-8 (cloth : alk. paper)
  ISBN 978-0-8014-7591-7 (pbk. : alk. paper)
  1. Affirmative action programs—Law and legislation—United States.
2. Affirmative action programs—United States. 3. Affirmative action programs in education—United States. I. Title.

  KF4755.5.S74   2009
  342.7308'5–dc22

2009007763

Cornell University Press strives to use environmentally responsible suppliers and materials to the fullest extent possible in the publishing of its books. Such materials include vegetable-based, low-VOC inks and acid-free papers that are recycled, totally chlorine-free, or partly composed of nonwood fibers. For further information, visit our website at www.cornellpress.cornell.edu.

Cloth printing   10 9 8 7 6 5 4 3 2 1
Paperback printing 10 9 8 7 6 5 4 3 2 1

To Charles Mills who inspired my work in this area

Contents

PREFACE

In 2003, I wrote a debate book on affirmative action with Carl Cohen of the University of Michigan. Cohen, a long time critic of affirmative action, had used the Freedom of Information Act to secure data about Michigan's affirmative action programs. He then gave this data to the Center for Individual Rights, which brought the lawsuits against the University of Michigan. This led to the U.S. Supreme Court's decisions in *Grutter v. Bollinger* and *Gratz v. Bollinger,* decisions that vindicated the Law School's affirmative action program but struck down the program used for undergraduates at the University.

I found writing the book with Cohen to be a wonderful exercise in public deliberation. We each wrote long essays defending our respective views. We then wrote detailed replies to each other's essays. I came away from this exercise seeing considerable common ground between our views. As I saw it, we each held the same individual-based view of remedial affirmative action, although we applied our shared view differently. Where we really differed was with respect to our assessment of nonremedial diversity

affirmative action. Cohen maintained that there were still more fundamental disagreements, but he only reached that conclusion by interpreting
my view in ways I have publicly repudiated, and for which, even after
repeated requests, he has been able to provide no textual support.

In 2006, my debate with Cohen and other critics of affirmative action,
such as William Allen of Michigan State University and past chair of the
U.S. Civil Rights Commission, entered a new phase when the Michigan Civil
Rights Initiative (MCRI)—a referendum that would rule out any race- and
sex-based affirmative action—was being discussed across the state. In debates in which I participated, Cohen and Allen repeatedly argued that the
passage of MCRI would not have negative impact on women or minorities
in Michigan. Now that MCRI has passed, and although its full impact has
yet to be assessed, undergraduate black enrollment at the University of
Michigan is down 22 percent from 2003.

In light of these developments, I think a new defense of affirmative action is needed. I also think it is important to document the level of racial
and sexual discrimination that exists in the United States and to offer a defense of an expanded diversity affirmative action program. Such a program
would include more preferences for economically disadvantaged applicants by cutting back on legacy and athletic preferences, which now benefit wealthy white applicants to elite colleges and universities. *Affirmative
Action for the Future* is my attempt to provide just this sort of a defense.

Many people have assisted me in writing this book. In particular, I thank
Carol Allen, William Allen, Elizabeth Anderson, Monica Bloomer, Carl
Cohen, Kristen Eliason, Neil Gotanda, Cheryl Harris, Jill Havey, Stephen
Kershnar, Janet Kourany, Bob Laird, Daniel Lipson, Michelle Moody-
Adams, Camila Morsch, Mark Nadel, Martha Nussbaum, David Oppen-
heimer, Marie-Christine Panwels, Paule Cruz Takash, John William
Templeton, Laurence Thomas, Richard Sander, Sonya Kourany Sterba,
Thomas Weisskopf, Christopher Westhoff, Celia Wolf-Devine, and Levon
Yuille. I also thank Oxford University Press for permission to draw mate-
rial from *Affirmative Action and Racial Preference* (2003) and Stanford University Press for permission to draw material from "Completing Thomas
Sowell's Study of Affirmative Action and Then Drawing Different Con-
clusions," *Stanford Law Review,* vol. 57, no. 2 (November 2004). I am also
grateful to Roger Haydon at Cornell University Press who believed in this
project from the beginning and kept after me to complete it.

Affirmative Action for the Future

INTRODUCTION

In *Grutter v. Bollinger* (2003)—the U.S. Supreme Court's most important decision on affirmative action—Justice Sandra Day O'Connor, writing for the majority, seemed to put a time constraint on the justification of race-based affirmative action. She ended her opinion with the claim "we expect that 25 years from now, the use of racial preferences will no longer be necessary to further the interest approved today."[1] Although at least one of her colleagues on the Court, Justice William Rehnquist, interpreted O'Connor's decision to mean that the Court's approval of race-based affirmative action will simply expire in 2028, this was not what O'Connor meant. In an interview given the day after the *Grutter* decision was announced, O'Connor clarified her view. What she meant was that "if we do our job on educating young people," then in twenty-five years we would no longer need race-based affirmative action.[2] Of course, O'Connor's view also implies that if we don't do our job and improve K through 12 education to provide virtually all U.S. school children with a quality education over this period, then there would be a justification for race-based affirmative action in the future.

The conditionality of O'Connor's justification for affirmative action is a quite common feature of other proposed justifications for affirmative action. In fact, virtually no one defends affirmative action under all circumstances. Usually, it is defended as the best alternative in a far-from-ideal set of circumstances.

It is also the case that opponents of affirmative action have a similar conditionality to their views. For example, Terence Pell, the president of the Center for Individual Rights—the group that has brought most of the lawsuits against affirmative action in the United States—is opposed to affirmative action because he thinks that in its absence people would have the "incentive to make the needed improvements to the elementary and secondary schools that are the source of the disparity in the first place."[3] Just as O'Connor's justification for affirmative action is empirically conditioned (presumably, we will know when we have provided a quality K through 12 education to all), so Pell's reason for rejecting affirmative action is also empirically conditioned. So if we put an end to affirmative action someplace (say, California) and the hypothesized good results for K though 12 education don't materialize, then we have proved that Pell's empirical grounds for rejecting affirmative action were false.

Conditionality enters into a discussion of affirmative action in other ways. For example, one of the common reasons offered for rejecting affirmative action is that racial and sexual discrimination is a thing of the past. Those who offer this reason for rejecting affirmative action clearly are expressing a conditionality with regard to their rejection of affirmative action. They do not reject affirmative action for all circumstances, but only for the circumstances they think presently obtain. If they are wrong that racial and sexual discrimination is a thing of the past, as I argue in chapter 1, then these opponents of affirmative action may actually turn into proponents. No one seriously engaged in this debate is absolutely in favor or absolutely against affirmative action.

The grounds for accepting or rejecting affirmative action are also rooted in, and conditional upon, an understanding of its history. That history is not very long. In the United States, it dates from the early 1960s, and in India from the early 1950s. In the United States, the history involves a rollercoaster ride with the Supreme Court, the Executive Branch, and

Congress taking different positions at different times, sometimes working together, sometimes working against each other. Without an understanding of this history, it is impossible to evaluate the current arguments being offered for and against affirmative action. Chapter 2 provides a brief account of the history on which the acceptance or rejection of affirmative action depends.

With respect to defining affirmative action, another and unfortunate conditionality manifests itself. Particular definitions are favored or rejected by some participants in the debate over affirmative action based on whether those definitions make the practice look good or make it look bad. Thus, proponents sometimes propose definitions of affirmative action, such as simply equating affirmative action with equal opportunity, that tend to make the practice obviously acceptable almost by definition. Similarly, opponents sometimes propose defining affirmative action as, say, reverse discrimination, which tends to make the practice obviously objectionable, again almost by definition.

Clearly, this way of conditionalizing definitions of affirmative action is question-begging and gets us nowhere. What we need to do is fashion a definition of affirmative action that does not simply presuppose the acceptable-ness or objectionable-ness of the practice. It would be a definition that both proponents and opponents of affirmative action can work with, one where proponents can claim to find examples or types of affirmative action that they then argue are defensible and where opponents can also claim to find examples or types that they then argue are objectionable. We need a definition where the various sides in the debate can contest the views of the others without being ruled out of court *by definition.* I claim to have provided just such a definition of affirmative action in chapter 3.

The definition proposed in chapter 3 also attempts to open up a possibility that previous definitions of affirmative action, including my own, have tended to exclude. The new definition allows that affirmative action can be based on race, or sex, *or* economic disadvantage. In the past, defenders of affirmative action have considered whether affirmative action based on economic disadvantage, also called "class-based affirmative action," could be justified. But this type of affirmative action usually was taken to be an alternative to race- or sex-based affirmative action. You either defended the one or you defended the other; you didn't defend them both. What I am proposing in chapter 3 is a broader definition that allows for programs of affirmative action to be compatibly based on race and sex as well as on economic disadvantage. Part of chapter 7 is devoted to a defense of just such a conception of affirmative action.

Conditionality enters the discussion of affirmative action in still another way. Arguments for and objections to affirmative action are not arguments and objections to all its forms. Rather they are arguments for and objections to particular types or subtypes of affirmative action. Most of the arguments for and objections can be grouped as applying to two types of affirmative action: remedial affirmative action and diversity affirmative action. (As I argue, each of these types also breaks down into two subtypes.)[4]

It is not always easy to keep separate these different arguments for and objections to different types and sub-types of affirmative action, and not infrequently both proponents and opponents get them confused. For example, an opponent might object to a particular example of affirmative action as if it were an example of remedial affirmative action when in fact it is an example of diversity affirmative action, thus making the objection irrelevant. Similarly, a proponent might try to argue for a particular practice of affirmative action on remedial grounds when it can be defended only on grounds of diversity, thus making the proposed argument useless. In chapters 4–7, I attempt to respect this conditionality of arguments for and objections to affirmative action by taking into account their limited applicability to particular types of affirmative action.

Finally, at least in the United States, proponents and opponents rarely recognize that the evaluation of affirmative action as practiced here is conditional upon an evaluation of the practice around the world. One opponent who has taken this conditionality to heart is Thomas Sowell at the Hoover Institution. In fact, Sowell more than anyone else has pioneered this way of evaluating affirmative action. He uses this approach to argue that an examination of affirmative action around the world provides the United States with good reason to terminate its own practice.[5] In Chapter 9, I try to show that Sowell's data from around the world fails to undercut the justification of affirmative action as practiced in the United States.

I have emphasized the conditionality and the resultant complexity involved in a proper evaluation of affirmative action in order to contrast it with the ballot initiative approach that Ward Connerly is currently sponsoring across the United States. Under Connerly's approach it is assumed that affirmative action can be appropriately addressed simply by asking voters whether they are for or against X (understood narrowly as race- and sex-based preferences, broadly as affirmative action). Such an approach does not provide any assessment of the arguments for or against particular types of X, and does not provide any assessment of the consequences of legally prohibiting X.[6] Surely, we can and should do better. What we clearly need is an open and fair evaluation of the various arguments for and objections to affirmative action. With this book, I hope to contribute to that endeavor.

1

Current Racial and Sexual Discrimination

Surveys in the United States today show that white Americans overwhelmingly publicly ascribe to principles of racial equality and integration.[1] At the same time, 80 percent of whites recently surveyed deny that racial discrimination against people of color is a significant problem.[2] In another survey, 70 percent of whites believe that blacks are treated equally in their communities. In this survey, 80 percent of whites also thought that underrepresented groups, such as blacks and Latinos, receive equal, if not preferred, treatment in education.[3] Another recent survey found that 68 percent of whites think that blacks have the same or more opportunities than whites to be "really successful and wealthy."[4] According to this survey, a majority of whites think that educationally the average black American is just as well off as, or better off than, the average white American; 47 percent think that blacks and whites enjoy the same standard of living. Still another survey found that most Americans believe that "reverse discrimination" is the predominant type of discrimination in the United States.[5]

Surprisingly, however, similar views were expressed in a poll taken in 1962, two years before the Civil Rights Act overcame a historic eighty-three-day filibuster in the Senate and made its way through the U.S. Congress. In that poll, more than nine in ten whites said that whites and blacks had just as good a chance for a quality education.[6] They said so even though at that time, despite two *Brown v. Board of Education* Supreme Court decisions, de jure segregation still held sway throughout most of the South. In the 1963–64 school year in the eleven states of the former Confederacy, only 1.17 percent of black students were attending schools with white students.[7]

Nevertheless, many today would hold that the view shared by a large majority of white Americans in 1962 was at the time fundamentally mistaken and grounded in underlying racial prejudice. But what about the views of the greater majority of white Americans today, as reflected in the surveys I have just cited? Might not they also be mistaken for somewhat similar reasons?

Consider the following data: in the United States today almost half of all black children live in poverty. Black unemployment is twice that of white, and the median net worth of white families is ten times that of black families. The infant mortality rate in many black communities is twice that of whites. Blacks are twice as likely as whites to be robbed, seven times more likely to be murdered or to die of tuberculosis. A male living in the Harlem neighborhood of New York City is less likely to reach age sixty-five than a resident of Bangladesh. According to a United Nations study, white Americans, when considered as a separate nation, rank first in the world in well-being (a measure that combines life expectancy, educational achievements, and income). African Americans rank twenty-seventh, and Hispanic Americans even lower at thirty-second.[8]

Yet these particular disparities between blacks and whites could be just the result of past discrimination. They do not necessarily provide evidence of current ongoing racial discrimination, although they do undercut the view that blacks and whites enjoy the same standard of living. Consider then the following data:

- According to a recent study of the U.S. Federal Reserve Board, the loan rejection rate for blacks in the highest income bracket is identical to the rejection rate of whites in the lowest income bracket. In another study, minority applicants are 50 percent more likely to be denied a loan than white applicants of equivalent economic status.[9]

- According to a study done at the University of Colorado at Boulder, blacks seeking business loans were two to three times more likely to be rejected than whites, and blacks were twelve times more likely to be rejected than whites at the highest levels of assets and collateral.[10]

- In a study by the Urban Institute equally qualified, identically dressed, white and African American applicants for jobs were used to test for bias in the job market for newspaper-advertised positions. White and African Americans were matched identically for age, work experience, speech patterns, personal characteristics, and physical build. The study found repeated discrimination against African American male applicants. The white men received three times as many job offers as equally qualified African Americans who interviewed for the same positions.[11]

- According to a 1998 study conducted by the Fair Housing Council in Washington, DC, minorities in the United States are discriminated against 40 percent of the time when they attempt to rent apartments or buy homes.[12]

- Another study revealed that African American and Hispanic American job applicants suffer blatant and easily identifiable discrimination one in every five times they apply for a job.[13]

- African American men with bachelor's degrees earn as much as $15,180 less than their white counterparts. Although native-born white males make up only 41 percent of the U.S. population, they comprise 80 percent of all tenured professors, 97 percent of all school superintendents, and 97 percent of senior managerial positions in Fortune 1000 industrial and Fortune 500 service companies. African Americans hold only 0.6 percent, Hispanic Americans 0.4 percent, and Asian Americans 0.3 percent of the senior managerial positions.[14]

- Many blacks are overqualified for the jobs they hold. It has been estimated that the failure to employ blacks in jobs for which they are overqualified resulted in a $241 billion loss to the U.S. economy in 1993.[15]

- In resume-only tests, whites were almost twice as likely as blacks to be blatantly preferred, despite their having less objective experience and fewer credentials.[16]

- In studies done in New York City and Milwaukee whites with prison records were more likely to be hired than black men without prison records.[17]

- A study of Bay area employment agencies found that white job applicants were preferred three times as often to equally matched black applicants.[18]

- One study done in the Los Angeles area found that race and skin color affected the probability of obtaining employment by as much as 52 percent.

Though whites and light-skinned African Americans were relatively likely to find employment when searching for a job, dark-skinned men were not. In fact, dark-skinned men were twice as likely as others to remain unemployed. According to another study only 10.3 percent of light-skinned African Americans men with thirteen or more years of schooling were unemployed, compared with 19.4 percent of their dark-skinned counterparts. Among men who had participated in job-training programs, light-skinned blacks actually had a lower jobless rate than their white counterparts—11.1 percent, compared with 14.5 percent. Yet the rate for dark-skinned African American men with job training was 26.8 percent.[19]

- The bipartisan Glass Ceiling Commission found that Asian American men earned between 83 and 90 percent of what white men with the same credentials earned. The figure was about 60 percent for Asian American women.[20]
- In elementary and high schools, according to a national study even when blacks demonstrate equal ability with whites, they are still far less likely to be placed in advanced classes. Even when children from lower income families, who are disproportionately of color, answer correctly all the math questions on a standardized test, it turns out that they are still less likely to be placed in advanced tracks than kids from upper income families who miss one-fourth of the questions on that test.[21]
- In a study of medical care racial and ethnic minorities were given poorer care than whites even when their income levels and insurance were the same.[22]
- Although blacks are more susceptible to kidney disease than whites, they are only half as likely as whites to be given a transplant, and those approved for a transplant have to wait twice as long as whites.[23]
- Blacks constitute about 13 percent of drug users in the United States but they make up 58 percent of those sent to prison for drug possession.[24] In Illinois, blacks are jailed for selling or using drugs at fifty-seven times the rate of whites.[25]
- Convicted murderers of whites are eleven times more likely to be condemned to death than convicted murders of blacks.[26] Although approximately 50 percent of murder victims each year are black, 80 percent of victims in death row cases are white and only 14 percent are black.[27]

There is also evidence of considerable race-based environmental inequities. Consider the following data:

- Penalties under hazardous waste laws at sites having the greatest white population were 500 percent higher than penalties at sites with the greatest minority population, averaging $335,566 in white areas, compared with $55,318 in minority areas.[28]

- The disparity under toxic waste law occurs by race and not by income. The average penalty in areas with the lowest median income is only 3 percent higher or lower than the average penalty in areas with the highest median income.[29]

- For all the federal environmental laws aimed at protecting citizens from air, water, and waste pollution, penalties in white communities were 46 percent higher than in minority communities.[30]

- Under the giant Superfund cleanup program, abandoned hazardous waste sites in minority areas take 20 percent longer to be placed on the national priority action list than those in white areas.[31]

- In Tacoma, Washington, where paper mills and other industrial polluters ruined the salmon streams and the way of life of a Native American tribe, the government did not include the tribe in assessing the pollution's impact on residents' health.[32]

- Three of every five African and Hispanic Americans live in a community with uncontrolled toxic waste sites.[33]

Surely, this data provides plenty of evidence that, at least in the United States, African Americans and other minorities currently experience considerable discrimination. Surely, this data also radically undercuts the view of the greater majority of white Americans today that racial discrimination is a thing of the past.

Unfortunately, in this respect white Americans today may not be all that different from their counterparts in 1962 despite the fact that they now judge their 1962 counterparts to have been grossly mistaken in their views. This is because white Americans today, or at least a majority of them, when faced with the hard-to-ignore evidence of current racial discrimination, have yet to reach a similar conclusion about their own views on the subject.

With respect to sexual discrimination, the situation is more difficult to assess because it is harder to find surveys indicating what the majority of men think about the prevalence of sexual discrimination in the United States. Yet there are a number of self-styled experts on gender relations— like Warren Farrell, author of the best-selling *The Myth of Male Power*— who argue that women have now achieved equality with men. According to these experts, the real problem we encounter today is that feminists want to push beyond equality to secure special advantages for women, which have the effect of discriminating against men.[34] Yet whether most men would agree with Farrell that it is now they who are primarily being discriminated against based on their sex, many men—especially after the nearly successful campaign of Hilary Clinton for the 2008 Democratic Party presidential nomination, would surely agree with Farrell that discrimination against women has become, for all practical purposes, a thing of the past.

Yet consider the following data:

- Comparing the annual income of full-time workers with four-year degrees or more, women in the United States earn, on average, only 72 cents for every dollar men earn. Put another way, a college-educated women working full-time earns $44,200 a year compared to $61,800 for her male counterpart—a difference of $17,600. For a woman working thirty years, the difference exceeds half a million dollars.[35] Moreover, if part-time workers are included in this comparison, the gap in the United States rises, with women earning only about half of what men earn.[36]
- Women now hold 70 percent of white-collar positions but only 10 percent of management positions. There are only two women CEOs in Fortune 1000 companies.[37]
- College-educated Hispanic women annually earn $1,600 less than white male high school graduates and nearly $16,000 less than college-educated white men. College-educated black women annually earn only $1,500 more than white male high school graduates and almost $13,000 less than college-educated white men.[38]
- College-educated white women earn only $3,000 more than white male high school graduates and $11,500 less than college-educated white men. Women with identical credentials are also promoted at approximately one-half the rate of their male counterparts.[39]
- A National Bureau of Economic Research project sent equally qualified pairs of male and female applicants to seek jobs at a range of Philadelphia restaurants. This "audit" found that high-priced restaurants offering good pay and tips were twice as likely to offer jobs to the male applicants over their equally qualified female counterparts.[40]

There is also a high incidence of sexual harassment in the workplace in the United States.

- In research conducted by psychologists 50 percent of women questioned in the workplace said they had been sexually harassed.[41]

- According to the U.S. Merit Systems Protection Board, within the federal government, 56 percent of 8,500 female civilian workers surveyed claimed to have experienced sexual harassment.[42]
- According to the *National Law Journal,* 64 percent of women in "pink-collar" jobs reported being sexually harassed and 60 percent of 3,000 women lawyers at 250 top law firms said that they had been harassed at some point in their careers.[43]
- In a survey by *Working Women* magazine 60 percent of high-ranking corporate women said they have been harassed; 33 percent more knew of others who had been.[44]
- Similarly, in a survey of 90,000 female soldiers, sailors, and pilots, 60 percent said they had been sexually harassed. Only 47 percent of the Army women surveyed said that they believed their leaders were serious about putting a stop to sexual harassment.[45]
- According to another study, 66 percent of women in the military experienced at least one form of sexual harassment in the past year.[46]
- Another study found that 50 percent of women at the U.S. Naval Academy, 59 percent at the U.S. Air Force Academy, and 76 percent at the U.S. Military Academy experienced some form of sexual harassment at least twice a month.[47]
- According to a 2002 study by the U.S. Department of Defense over 60 percent of women in the military experienced some type of sexual harassment, down from 78 percent in 1995.[48]

There have also been legal cases brought for sexual harassment where large settlements have been paid out. For example, in 1998 Dupont Corporation paid out $3.53 million in a jury award to a peroxide departmental operator who was driven out of her job because of her sex. In 2002, the New York City Police Department paid $1.85 million in a jury award to a police officer who was forced out in retaliation for a sexual harassment complaint. In 2004, Home Depot paid a $5.5 million settlement to an employee for hostile environment sexual harassment and retaliation.[49]

There is plenty of evidence that women have also been neglected in medical research. For example, the Multiple Risk Factor Intervention Trial (MR. FIT)—a study to evaluate the impact of various activities on the risk of heart attack—was conducted with 12,866 men and 0 women. Other examples include the Health Professionals Follow-Up Study examining the relation of coffee consumption and heart disease, which was done with 45,589 men and 0 women; and the Physicians' Health Study on the effects of aspirin on the risk of heart attack, which was done with 22,071 male but no female physicians.[50] In addition, women had not been included in drug trials in the United States, even though they consume roughly 80 percent of pharmaceuticals. Drugs such as Valium were not tested on women, even though 2 million women took the drug each year.[51]

The General Accounting Office report found that fewer than half of publicly available prescription drugs in the United States had been analyzed for gender-related differences in response.[52] As a result, frequently prescribed drugs and dosages were based on men's conditions and average weights and metabolisms. This led to twice as many adverse reactions to drugs in women as in men.[53] For example, some clot-dissolving drugs that are useful for treating heart attacks in men were found to cause bleeding problems in women, and some drugs that are commonly used to treat high blood pressure tended to lower men's mortality from heart attack while raising women's. Other drugs (for example, antidepressants) varied in their effects over the course of a women's menstrual cycle such that a constant dosage of an antidepressant may be too high at some points in a woman's cycle and too low at others. Still other drugs (for example, acetaminophen, an ingredient in many pain relievers) are eliminated in women at slower rates than they are eliminated in men. Not only were drugs developed for men that turned out to be potentially dangerous for women, but also drugs that were potentially beneficial for women may have been eliminated in early testing because the test group did not include women.[54]

Similar problems plagued AIDS research. As late as 1991, neither of the two U.S. institutions that distributed funds for AIDS research had funded a major project to address whether women with AIDS experienced different symptoms than men.[55] As a result, the official definition of AIDS did not originally include many of the HIV-related conditions in women because what was known about the disease was derived principally from research on men. In fact, most early studies on women were largely restricted to preventing the transmission of HIV from mother to child.[56] This resulted in little information on the progress of the disease in women themselves. Consequently, most health-care workers were unable to diagnose AIDS in women until the disease had advanced significantly. On average, men died thirty months after diagnosis, while women died only fifteen weeks after diagnosis.[57] All of this data surely indicates that women are still being discriminated against in a variety of ways.[58]

It is in the face of this considerable evidence of existing racial and sexual discrimination that we now turn to the question of the justification for affirmation action. One of the reasons frequently offered for rejecting affirmative action is that racial and sexual discrimination is a thing of the past, and so affirmative action is no longer needed. Confronted with all the evidence of existing racial and sexual discrimination surveyed in this chapter, we know that this reason for rejecting affirmative action is not credible. Of course, there may be other telling reasons against affirmative action, but it is important to recognize that as we now turn to the question of whether affirmative action can be justified, by first examining the history of the practice, we do so for a society where various forms of racial and sexual discrimination are still widespread.

2

A Legal History of Race- and Sex-Based Affirmative Action

Race- and Sex-Based Affirmative Action in the United States

The first use of the phrase "affirmative action" in the United States is commonly attributed to Executive Order 10925, issued by President John Kennedy in 1961.[1] Two years later, when Kennedy proposed the legislation that became the Civil Rights Act of 1964, he and leading liberals of the 1960s assumed that by simply banning discrimination government could create a level playing field where equal opportunity prevailed. It was an assumption that they borrowed from baseball, where Jackie Robinson and other black players had eventually thrived once racial barriers were removed, and from school desegregation cases in the South that were successful in dismantling dual educational systems.

The Civil Rights Act of 1964 prohibits any employer from discriminating because of an "individual's race, color, religion, sex, or national origin." The act also requires that "no person in the United States shall, on the grounds of race, color, or national origin, be excluded from participation in, be denied the benefits of, or be subjected to discrimination under any program or activity receiving Federal financial assistance." This feature of the act proved to be especially important to its implementation.

To secure passage of the Civil Rights Act of 1964 over a southern filibuster that consumed a record eighty-three working days, it was necessary to deprive the Equal Employment Opportunity Commission (EEOC) of cease-and-desist authority as well as the power to sue. Accordingly, the EEOC was initially left with the task of being a conciliator.

Sixteen days after the act was passed, a riot erupted in Harlem in response to an alleged incident of police brutality. The following week, riots erupted in Brooklyn and Rochester. That summer also saw riots in Philadelphia; Jersey City, Paterson and Elizabeth, New Jersey; and Dixmoor, Illinois. But these were nothing compared to what was to come the following summer in the Watts section of southern Los Angeles. The riot in Watts lasted six days. Thirty-four people were killed, 1,072 injured (the vast majority black), over 4,000 arrested, and 977 buildings destroyed or damaged. These and other riots (290 just between 1966 and 1968, according to one study) formed the background against which the Civil Rights Act of 1964 was initially implemented.

To implement the act, President Lyndon Johnson issued Executive Order 11246, which required that "each executive department and agency shall establish and maintain a positive program of equal employment opportunity."[2] In response, the Department of Labor created an Office of Federal Compliance Program (OFCP) to implement Section VI of the act. This left the EEOC with the core responsibility of enforcing a private right of nondiscrimination under Section VII by responding administratively to individual complaints. By 1967, the EEOC had received almost 15,000 complaints. Of these, 6,040 had been earmarked for investigation, and the tiny agency's overwhelmed investigators had completed inquiries on only 3,319. The EEOC achieved conciliation with respect to only 110 cases (involving 330 complaints).[3] By 1968, its complaint backlog exceeded 30,000. A decade later, that number had grown to 150,000.[4] In recent years, the EEOC has received about 63,000 complaints annually and has been able to bring suit in no more than 500 a year.[5] Moreover, cases take the better part of a decade or more to reach a legal resolution.[6]

As the EEOC was taking on its conciliatory role under the Civil Rights Act of 1964, the Department of Labor's OFCP began collecting employment records by race and using them to evaluate hiring practices.[7] It also started a program by which contractors who had received government contracts would be required to demonstrate that they were prepared to meet affirmative action obligations. As this program was to be applied in Philadelphia (where there was only 1 percent minority membership in the craft unions and 30 percent minority membership in the construction trade), those who had received government contracts had to "provide in detail for specific steps to guaranteed equal employment opportunity keyed to the problems and needs of minority groups... for the prompt achievement of full and equal opportunity."[8] During Johnson's administration, however, the Philadelphia Program ran into difficulty with the General Accounting Office for introducing further requirements after contracts were awarded. There was also the worry that the program's affirmative action requirements would run afoul of the Civil Rights Act's prohibition of quotas.

A revised Philadelphia Program was put forward during the Nixon administration, which specified its affirmative action requirements in terms of a target "range" of minorities (for 1970, it was 4 to 9 percent) that the contractor would try to meet. The program was able to eventually withstand a federal district court challenge that it was employing quotas. Moreover, because there were no negotiations after bids were opened in the revised Philadelphia Program, the U.S. Congress determined that the plan was able to meet the objection of the comptroller general. The success of the Philadelphia Program led the Nixon administration to issue a new set of affirmative action guidelines that now applied to all government contractors with fifty or more employees and at least $50,000 in government business. The guidelines required contractors to take into consideration "the percentage of the minority work force as compared with the total work force in the immediate labor areas," and based on that ratio, to design "specific goals and timetables" to correct any hiring problems.[9]

These actions of the OFCP were clearly more effective at improving the situation of minorities than those the EEOC was able to achieve through its conciliatory approach. Moreover, the U.S. Congress had a chance, in the Civil Rights Act of 1972, to turn back the racial preference policies adopted by the OFCP (specific amendments were offered to that effect), but it refused to do so.[10] In fact, Congress extended the requirements of the act to state and local governments. Nevertheless, visitors to government contractors in 1994–95 who inquired about their compliance with affirmative action requirements found that 75 percent were in substantial non-compliance. In fact, since 1972 only forty-one contractors in the United States have been debarred from the list of approved federal contractors out of the thousands whose performance was judged unsatisfactory. In addition, only four of those who have been debarred were large corporations, with the debarment lasting less than three months.[11] One study found that most agencies responsible for nonconstruction contractors reviewed less than 20 percent of all federal contracts. One local office had two people monitoring 29,000 contracts.[12] Overall, there were only enough compliance officers to review about 4,000 contractors annually, meaning that, at best, reviews could be done perhaps once every forty-six years for each company.[13]

Relevant U.S. Supreme Court Cases

The first U.S. Supreme Court decision relevant to affirmative action was *Griggs v. Duke Power Company* (1971). In *Griggs,* the African American petitioners argued that their rights under Title VII of the Civil Rights Act had been violated because Duke Power used criteria for hiring and promotion that adversely affected them but were unrelated to job performance. In an eight-to-zero decision, the Court agreed. That was the one and only unanimous decision by the Supreme Court on affirmative action. However, a later Supreme Court with different members overturned this very decision with a five-to-four vote.

The issue of affirmative action in education was first addressed in *DeFunis v. Odegaard* (1974). The Court decided that the case was moot because by the time the decision was rendered DeFunis—the student who had been denied admission to the University of Washington law school—had already been admitted to the law school and was just about to complete his degree. It was only in *Regents of the University of California v. Bakke* (1978) that the U.S. Supreme Court addressed the issue of affirmative action in education on its merits, and there the Court significantly restricted its practice. In that decision, a majority found both the use of quotas in the affirmative action program of the Davis medical school and the school's goal of remedying the effects of societal discrimination to be in violation of the Civil Rights Act and the equal protection clause of the Fourteenth Amendment of the U.S. Constitution. However, a different majority (with only Justice Powell as the common member) seemed to allow that taking

race and ethnicity into account as a factor to achieve diversity does not violate the equal protection clause of the Fourteenth Amendment.

Thus, the legal effect of the *Bakke* decision was to still allow affirmative
action programs in education, but to significantly limit the way that they
could be practiced and justified. The *Bakke* decision also required strict
scrutiny of any race-based affirmative action program in education, meaning it was only permitted if it was narrowly tailored to meet a compelling
government interest. This constraint was taken to be required by the equal
protection clause. However, the same U.S. Congress that passed the Fourteenth Amendment in 1867 also passed race-conscious statutes providing
schools and farmland to both free blacks and former slaves, which do not
appear to satisfy the constraints that the *Bakke* majority found implicit in
the Fourteenth Amendment. It is therefore difficult to see how the constraints on the use of racial classifications imposed by the *Bakke* decision
could be grounded in the Fourteenth Amendment as that amendment was
understood by those who enacted it. What we have here is a new understanding of the Fourteenth Amendment, whereby it is no longer utilized
to protect blacks from racial domination and discrimination by the white
majority but rather primarily to protect the white majority from governmental action that favors blacks and other minorities.

Following the *Bakke* decision, came a number of U.S. Supreme Court
cases concerning affirmative action in employment. In *United Steelworkers
of America v. Weber* (1979), a majority of the Court found that a voluntary
affirmative action program requiring a temporary quota to eliminate traditional patterns of conspicuous racial segregation was permissible under
Title VII of the Civil Rights Act of 1964. In one particular plant where the
program was to he applied, the craft workforce was less than 2 percent African American, even though the local workforce was 39 percent African
American. In *Fullilove v. Klutznick* (1980), the Supreme Court found that
a congressional affirmative action program that required that 10 percent
of a federal grant for public works projects be used to procure the services
of minority business enterprises did not violate equal protection under the
Fifth or Fourteenth Amendments or the Civil Rights Act of 1964. The
Court judged the program to be within Congress's power to attempt to
eradicate what it determines to be the effects of past discrimination. At the
time, it was noted that only 1 percent of all federal procurement was concluded by minority business enterprises, although minorities comprised

15 to 18 percent of the population. Nine years later, however, the Court, with three new conservative appointees—Sandra Day O'Connor, Antonin Scalia, and Anthony Kennedy—reversed itself, ruling in *City of Richmond v. J. A. Croson CO.* (1989) against Richmond's similar affirmative action program. In *Wygant v. Jackson Board of Education* (1986), the Supreme Court further required that any institution that sought to compensate for past discrimination must be guilty of that same discrimination in the past.

When Ronald Reagan became President of the United States in 1981, he made sure that his key civil rights appointees shared his opposition to affirmative action. To run the EEOC, Reagan selected future Supreme Court Justice Clarence Thomas, a specialist in the unrelated field of tax law, who did not hesitate to describe himself as "unalterably opposed to programs that force or even cajole people to hire a certain percentage of minorities." Between 1981 and 1983, the budgets of the EEOC and the OFCCP (the Office of Federal Contract Compliance Program) were respectively cut by 10 and 24 percent, their staffs by 12 and 34 percent, and travel funds for EEOC investigations were eliminated.[14] During the Reagan era, affirmative action under the federal government's contract compliance program virtually ceased to exist.

In *Wards Cove Packing Company v. Atonio* (1989), the U.S. Supreme Court again reversed itself, this time rejecting its earlier *Griggs v. Duke Power Company* decision (1971), which had held that employers were ultimately responsible for showing the "business necessity" of any employment practice that was shown to have discriminatory impact on minorities. In this new decision, the Court held that it was the employees who had to prove discriminatory intent in such cases, something that is very difficult to do. This decision, however, ultimately sparked a legislative response in the form of the Civil Rights Act of 1991. Initially, President George H. W. Bush opposed the act, calling it a "quota bill," and vetoed an earlier version.[15] But in the wake of the public debate over Anita Hill's charge that Clarence Thomas—Bush's Supreme Court nominee—had sexually harassed her, Bush's options became limited, and he signed the bill into law. This new civil rights act shifted the burden of proof in disparate-impact cases back to the employer. It required a company with an employment practice that resulted in disparate impact on minorities to demonstrate that its practice was both "job related" and "consistent with business necessity."

With Clarence Thomas taking Thurgood Marshall's seat, the U.S. Supreme Court sought to impose further restrictions on affirmative action. In *Adarand Constructors v. Pena* (1995), the Court, in a five-to-four decision, struck down two of its earlier decisions, ruling that a standard of strict scrutiny applied to race-based action by the federal as well as state and local government.[16] This meant that in both areas race-based actions must be able to satisfy a demanding review in order to be relevant to any constitutionally acceptable purpose. The Court also held that its standard of review "is not dependent on the race of those burdened or benefited by a particular (race-based) classification." Justice O'Connor denied that this now meant that affirmative action was to be equated with invidious discrimination (or as Justice Stevens put it in his dissent, that a welcome mat was to be equated with a "No Trespassing" sign). Justices Thomas and Scalia, for their part, endorsed this identification. In Thomas's words, "government-sponsored racial discrimination based on benign prejudice is just as noxious as discrimination inspired by malicious prejudice." In Thomas's view, an affirmative action program that reduces white candidates chances of admission to a particular elite college or university by one half of one percent (the estimated effect of eliminating existing affirmative action programs) is no different from a Jim Crow laws that prohibited all black candidates from even attending that school—surely an equivalence that strains the imagination.[17]

Other Legal Developments

In *Hopwood v. Texas* (1996), the U.S. Court of Appeals for the Fifth Circuit argued that an educational institution can only justifiably implement an affirmative action program if it is designed simply to correct for the past discrimination of that very institution. The goal of educational diversity was also no longer judged sufficient to justify an affirmative action program.[18] In response to *Hopwood,* the Texas State Legislature passed a law requiring the University of Texas at Austin and Texas A&M University to admit all applicants who graduated in the top 10 percent of their high school class. By 1999, under this 10 Percent Plan, undergraduate enrollment at the University of Texas at Austin was as diverse as the last class enrolled prior to the *Hopwood* decision (1996). At the University of Texas School of Law, the percentage of the entering class that was African American dropped from 5.8 percent (29 students) in 1996 to 0.9 percent (6 students) in 1997.[19] American Indian enrollment at the law school dropped from 1.2 percent (6 students) in 1996 to 0.2 percent (1 student) in 1997.[20] Hispanic enrollment dropped from 9.2 percent (46 students) in 1996 to 6.7 percent (31 students) in 1997.[21] Although there has been some improvement in more recent years, enrollment of African Americans has yet to approach pre-*Hopwood* levels.

In the same year that the *Hopwood* decision took effect in Texas, voters in California approved Proposition 209, called the California Civil Rights Initiative.[22] It amended the state's constitution so as to rule out "preferential treatment to any individual or group on the basis of race, sex, color or national origins." Earlier in 1995, following intense lobbying by the then governor Pete Wilson, the University of California Board of Regents voted to end racial preferences in its university system. In 2001, however, the California Regents reversed themselves, rescinding their earlier ban on racial preferences. That same year, California began admitting the top 4 percent of each high school in the state regardless of the students' SAT scores, provided that they had taken certain required courses. Consequently, the University of California system admitted 18.6 percent black, Hispanic, and American Indians first year undergraduates for the fall 2001, just shy of 1997's 18.8 percent, the last time racial preferences were used in admissions.[23]

At the same time, a significant disparity can still be found at the system's flagship campuses of UCLA and Berkeley as well as at the state's professional schools. In 1996, before Proposition 209 took effect in California, there were eighty-nine Hispanic Americans, forty-three African Americans, and ten American Indians enrolled as first year students at the top three University of California law schools. In 1997, these numbers fell to fifty-nine, sixteen, and four, respectively. At Berkeley, only one African American enrolled in the freshman law class in 1997, while there had been twenty enrolled the year before.[24]

On June 23, 2003, the Supreme Court handed down two decisions on diversity affirmative action in *Grutter v. Bollinger* and *Gratz v. Bollinger.* Both decisions were passed by a majority that held that it is constitutionally permissible to use racial preferences to achieve the educational benefits of diversity. In *Grutter,* the majority further approved the University of Michigan Law School's way of achieving those benefits. In *Gratz,* the majority rejected the university's way of achieving those benefits for its undergraduate program. (These cases are discussed in more detail in chapter 7.)

Responding to the *Grutter* decision, on July 8, 2003, a small band of Michigan residents led by Ward Connerly from California gathered on the front steps of the University of Michigan's Harlan Hatcher Graduate Library to launch the Michigan Civil Rights Initiative (MCRI), modeled after California's Proposition 209.[25] Those proposing this amendment to the Michigan Constitution formulated it in terms of a ban on the use of race- and sex-based preferences rather than as a ban on affirmative action to achieve equal opportunity for women and minorities. Thereby they secured a description of their proposed change to the Michigan constitution that Michigan voters would be more likely to endorse. Carl Cohen, a professor of philosophy at the University of Michigan was the first to sign the petition to place MCRI on the 2004 ballot followed by Jennifer Gratz and Barbara Gutter, two of the named litigants in the Michigan cases.

More than 200 bipartisan, statewide, local and national organizations and political leaders, including the Catholic Council, the National Organization for Women, Michigan's Democratic governor Jennifer Granholm and her Republican opponent Dick DeVos, former president Gerald Ford, and former secretary of state Colin Powell came together to oppose MCRI. Legal challenges to the initiative, its formulation, and its supporting signatures all delayed its appearance on the ballot until November 2006.[26]

In fall of 2004, William Allen—a law professor at Michigan State University and former member and chair of the U.S. Commission on Civil Rights during the Reagan years—and Barbara Grutter met with several members of MCRI's steering committee, including Jennifer Gratz and Leon Drocet. They discussed the possibility of putting a "Michigan black face" on the campaign by having Allen join the MCRI team in a leadership role. When Gratz and Connerly showed little interest in making such a change, Grutter and Allen together with Allen's wife, Carol, decided to form their own organization officially named "A Fair Michigan" (with "Toward a Fair Michigan" [TAFM] as an alternate name). Its proclaimed purpose was to provide "a civic forum for a fair and open exchange of views on the question of affirmative action, and to support organizations similarly disposed."[27]

Once legally constituted TAFM began to solicit funds, organize debates on affirmative action, and operate a website that provided answers to various questions on affirmative action from different perspectives. However, the organization fell short of its stated objectives. First, although TAFM claimed to be interested in creating a fair and open exchange of views about affirmative action, only supporters of the Michigan Initiative were included on its board of directors. Second, the TAFM website purported to provide diverse answers to fifty-four questions about affirmative action. However, Allen was permitted to answer fifty-one and Carl Cohen thirty-one, while the two opponents of MCRI who were permitted to answer the most questions, Thomas Weisskopf and Elizabeth Anderson, were only allowed to answer thirty and sixteen questions, respectively.[28] Clearly, this did not provide a very fair balance of different perspectives.

Nevertheless, in many of the debates sponsored by TAFM across Michigan, one question kept recurring: Wouldn't the impact of the MCRI on Michigan be similar to the impact of Proposition 209 on California? Not too surprisingly, both sides tended to agree that the impacts would be similar, but then they disagreed about how to characterize the impact Proposition 209 had on California. On the one hand, opponents of MCRI cited a report by Susan Kaufmann, associate director of the Center for the Education of Women at the University of Michigan, that claimed that since 1996, the year Proposition 209 took effect, the percentage of women in the construction trades in California in an expanding market had dropped by one-third, while outside of California, it increased across the nation.[29] On the other hand, proponents of MCRI, although criticizing other less important aspects of the Kaufmann report, simply failed to address this central claim about the negative impact on women resulting from the limitations Proposition 209 placed on outreach affirmative action.[30]

Opponents of MCRI also pointed out that the enrollment of blacks and Latinos is still down significantly at the elite University of California schools. For instance, the year before Proposition 209 took effect, there were 260 first-year black students enrolled at Berkeley. In 2005, there were only 108, and not one black was admitted to the first-year engineering class. Moreover, the graduation rate of minorities admitted after Proposition 209 was the same as it was before.[31] So, for almost ten years, Berkeley had been graduating only half as many blacks each year, as it had before Proposition 209, and the whole university was deprived of the educational benefits of diversity these additional blacks would have brought to the school. Similarly, before Proposition 209 took effect, the first-year class at UCLA included 221 black students, whereas in 2006 there were only 100.[32] Proponents of MCRI countered by pointing out that the overall enrollment of minorities in California's higher education system had now rebounded after the passage of Proposition 209, conceding that enrollment at the more elite schools still significantly lagged behind pre-Proposition 209 levels.[33]

Unfortunately, proponents of MCRI failed to appreciate the implications of their concession. As Justice Sandra O'Connor put it in her majority opinion in the *Grutter* case, "In order to cultivate a set of leaders with legitimacy in the eyes of the citizenry, it is necessary that the path to leadership be visibly open to talented and qualified individuals of every race and ethnicity." Yet given that only a handful of elite law schools account for twenty-five of one hundred U.S. Senators, seventy-four U.S. Court of Appeals judges, and nearly two hundred of the more than six hundred U.S. District Court judges, and given that 50 percent of the top 1,000 CEOs are graduates from the 10 elite universities, limiting enrollment of underrepresented minorities at elite schools of higher education in California, or Michigan, or anywhere in the United States cannot help but produce negative results.[34]

In spite of the negative data from California, MCRI was approved by Michigan voters (58-42). This was despite the fact that polls of likely voters taken in the weeks and days immediately preceding the vote consistently indicated a dead heat. In the final weeks before the vote, the initiative may have been drowned out by other concerns. Although about $7 million was spent on MCRI, an unprecedented $60 million was spent on the governor's race taking up much of the air-time in those final weeks, plus the state's Detroit Tigers were playing in the World Series.[35] It could also be that the way the initiative was deceptively formulated may have been the deciding factor. In any case, Michigan residents now have to live with the consequences, and similar initiatives are in the works in a number of other states.

Nevertheless, MCRI might have never come up to a vote if the state and federal authorities had acted, or been empowered to act, on the considerable evidence of fraud in the gathering of the signatures needed to put it on the ballot. There were repeated instances where canvassers for signatures represented MCRI as a referendum that was designed "to keep affirmative action," as a "pro-civil rights and pro-affirmative action" and as a "to help black kids get to college" referendum.[36] Unless a prospective signer who was approached noticed a five-word phrase that prohibited "preferential treatment" that was embedded in the small print of a 337-word amendment and knew that "preferential treatment" for all practical purposes meant "affirmative action," he or she would not know that the proposed referendum was in any way related to (banning) affirmative action.[37] Scripts instructed canvassers to ask registered voters, "Do you believe in affirmative action? If so, we need to work together to save it by putting it on the ballot in November. Please help keep affirmative action alive. We need you to sign now."[38]

The Michigan Civil Rights Commission reported that the canvassers targeted African American citizens on a statewide basis by carefully selecting "locations where it would be expected that a large number of supporters of affirmative action would congregate, such as churches and community gatherings in African American neighborhoods," thus obtaining at least 125,000 of the 508,000 signatures.[39] The Michigan Secretary of State reviewed a randomly selected sample of 500 signatures gathered, and then reported the fraud charges to the State Board of Canvassers. When the board attempted to look into these charges, it was told by the Michigan Appeals Court that it did not have the authority to do so. The Michigan Civil Rights Commission continued to investigate the charges and concluded that the fraud revealed in its hearings was "just the tip of the iceberg," claiming that there "is substantial credible testimony that MCRI's efforts to change the Constitution of the State of Michigan rest on a foundation of fraud and misrepresentation."[40]

The matter was then taken to Federal District Court. The District Court concluded that the MCRI campaign "engaged in systematic voter fraud" and it admonished the Michigan State Courts, the Board of Canvassers, the Secretary of State, the Attorney General, and Bureau of Elections for not taking the "allegations of voter fraud seriously."[41] The only law relevant at the federal level was the Voting Rights Act, which required that the fraud be directed at minority voters before action could be taken. Because the federal court judged that the fraud was against all Michigan voters, and because there is no federal anti-fraud statute, the federal court could do nothing. Though the state courts and the Michigan Secretary of State presumably had the power to investigate and act against the fraud, they did not do so. Thus, the MCRI went to the voters without any state or federal agency, with the requisite authority, reviewing its seemingly fraudulent origins.[42]

When June 2006 the U.S. Supreme Court agreed to hear two cases appealing school integration decisions in Washington and Kentucky. The possibility arose that the newly constituted Court, especially with Samuel Alito having replaced Sandra O'Connor, might be interested in overturning the *Grutter* decision, thus providing another victory for the opponents of affirmative action. During the previous year, with Justice O'Connor still on the Court, the justices had refused to hear a similar case from Lynn, Massachusetts, but now, reversing itself, the Court expressed its willingness to hear the cases from Washington and Kentucky.

In its decision in *Parents Involved in Community v. Seattle School District* and in *Meredith v. Jefferson County Board of Education,* the Supreme Court did not overturn the *Grutter* decision. The Court did significantly reduce the ability of school districts, K through 12, to use race as a way to promote integration. The Jefferson County, Kentucky, school district had classified students as black or "other" in order to make certain elementary school assignments and to rule on transfer requests, and the Seattle school district has used race as a tiebreaker to allocate slots in particular schools. In its plurality decision, the Court found that these particular uses of race by the school districts were not sufficiently narrowly tailored to achieve a compelling government interest.

Justice Kennedy, in particular, criticized the districts for conceptualizing and implementing their race-based means for assigning students to particular schools in an imprecise way. He also criticized the districts for not exploring other less explicitly race-based means like strategic site selections of new schools, drawing attendance zones with general recognition of neighborhood demographics, and allocating resources for special programs to certain schools. The Court claimed that these school districts had failed to distinguish the racial integration that they professed to endorse from the goal of racial proportionality that the Court had rejected in the past in the absence of proven discrimination.

In some respects this decision by the Court is similar to the *Bakke* decision on affirmative action with Justice Kennedy, like Justice Powell before him, representing the swing vote in the plurality decision. An important difference here is that Powell, unlike Kennedy, presented a fairly clear way for schools to proceed in order to respect the Court's limitation on race-based strategies. Unfortunately, one of the alternatives that Kennedy proposed—redrawing attendance zones—has proven even less popular with parents, another—site selections of schools—runs into the problem that racially integrated neighborhoods are usually in transition, and the third—magnet schools—has proved to be insufficient. So it isn't clear what workable alternatives school districts that are seeking racial integration have. More work, however, does need to be done to specify an educationally based standard of racial integration and to show how such a standard is distinct, yet possibly practically related, to certain kinds of racial proportionalism. For example, it may be that a certain standard of racial integration is ideal, but given the demographics of a particular school district, only less ideal racial proportionalism is all that is practically feasible.

In any case, there is a noteworthy contrast between the way the Supreme Court, especially in recent years, has been so restrictive on the use of racial classifications in affirmative action, and the way that the Court and other higher organs of the U.S. Government have been so accepting of virtually unlimited detention and torture of so-called enemy combatants (in some cases, U.S. citizens) and unlimited searches without warrants of communications going in and out of the United States. Could the one means be objectionable while the others are unobjectionable?

With respect to affirmative action and racial integration, there is considerable public evidence of the benefits of these policies. With respect to the U.S. government's enemy combatant policy, its policy on torture and warrantless searches of communications, there is little or no public evidence of any benefits and, in fact, considerable public evidence that these policies have led to widespread harm.[43] Yet the Court has been extremely restrictive in the one case and, together with other higher organs of the U.S. Government, has imposed virtually no restrictions in the other. The almost complete lack of a justification for the latter policies further undermines whatever presumed justification there was for the former policies. Unfortunately, it has been easier, and more plausible, to believe that the same pattern of injustice in the U.S. government infects both sets of policies.

Outside the United States

There are a number of interesting similarities and differences between affirmative action as practiced in the United States and as practiced elsewhere in the world. In India, affirmative action, which is called reservation, was endorsed following its independence by constitutional convention in 1950–51, making it the longest continually functioning such effort in the world. The very first amendment to the Indian constitution empowered the state to make "any special provision for the advancement of any socially and educationally backward class of citizens or the Scheduled Castes and the Scheduled Tribes." The Scheduled Castes are the Hindu untouchables, constituting about 15 percent of the population, and the Scheduled Tribes are geographically isolated groups with aboriginal cultural features, constituting 7.5 percent of the population. The constitutional convention left it to special commissions and the central government to determine who belonged to the socially and educationally backward classes, popularly referred to as Other Backward Classes. Reservation quotas of 15 percent for Scheduled Castes and 7.5 percent for Scheduled Tribes were immediately enacted by the central government for jobs and places at educational institutions under its control. State governments enacted similar reservations. No reservation was originally envisaged for the Other Backward Classes with respect to the central government, but each state government was left free to make such reservations as it saw fit.

Two national commissions in India attempted to specify who should belong to the Other Backward Classes in social and economic terms rather than in terms of caste, but neither was able to do so. The second commission, the Mandal Commission, specified 3,743 castes, malting up 52 percent of India's population, as belonging to the Other Backward Classes. The Mandal Commission recommended a 27 percent reservation for those who belonged to those classes. The central government accepted this recommendation in 1991. More recently, an additional preference has been given to those who are most economically disadvantaged within each of these three general caste-based categories of backward classes.

Affirmative action in Malaysia dates from 1969, when Malay natives went on a rampage against ethnic Chinese immigrants in Kuala Lumpur, leaving 196 people dead, three-quarters of them Chinese. Following the riots, the government launched an affirmative action program with two goals: to wipe out poverty regardless of race, and to restructure society so that no ethnic group could be identified with a specific set of jobs. The results have been impressive. The incidence of poverty has plunged from 74 percent of Malays in 1970 to 6 percent in 1994, and Malays now constitute 64 percent of the students at public universities. The Malay share of national wealth has also soared from about 1.5 percent in 1969 to 19.4 percent in 1998; but the ethnic Chinese share has also increased from 22.8 percent to 38.5 percent. The main losers have been foreigners, whose share has plunged.

In South Africa, progress through affirmative action programs in both the public and the private sectors has been fairly rapid following the rise to power of the African National Congress under the leadership of Nelson Mandela in 1994. So far, more than one million black South Africans have moved from poverty to the middle class, primarily because of affirmative action job opportunities. In 1995, the University of Witwatersrand, long known for its promotion of racial diversity, for the first time admitted more black than white students. Nevertheless, women have been ignored in most affirmative action programs in South Africa, where women of all races are still prohibited from opening bank accounts or entering into business contracts without their husbands' permission. Although the government did create a Commission on Women's Emancipation to study the problem, it appointed a man to head the commission.

Conversely, the Court of Justice of the European Union in *Marschall v. Land Nordrhein-Westfalen* (1997) has ruled in favor of affirmative action for women where there are fewer women than men in a particular occupational bracket, "unless reasons specific to an individual male candidate tilt the balance in his favor." This decision permits an even stronger preference for women than that allowed by the U.S. Supreme Court in *Johnson v. Transportation Agency of Santa Clara County* (1986), which limits a preference for women to traditionally segregated workplaces.

So we can see that affirmative action programs in India, Malaysia, and South Africa are much more extensive than those in the United States, and that the European Union now has a broader legal basis for affirmative action for women than the United States.

3

How Best to Define
Affirmative Action

The degree to which people in general are in favor of affirmative action largely depends on how that policy is described. For example, a *Los Angeles Times* poll showed that 58 percent of African Americans "opposed special preferences based on race and not merit," and a *Washington Post*/ABC poll showed that roughly two out of three women "oppose preferential treatment for women." On the other hand, according to pollster Lou Harris, every poll that has asked the simple question as to whether people "favor or oppose affirmative action—without strict quotas" has obtained a similar result: people favor affirmative action. Support runs 55 percent in favor to 40 percent against in more recent polls down from the average majority of 60 percent in favor to 38 percent against in polls taken over the past twenty-five years. Moreover, when people in California were asked whether they would still favor Proposition 209 if it outlawed all affirmative action programs for women and minorities, its support dropped to 30 percent and the number of those opposed rose to 56 percent. In addition, when asked about affirmative action programs at their workplaces, 80 percent of Euro-American workers strongly support the programs they know about and that directly affect them. According to another study, affirmative action programs were less palatable when they were applied to African Americans and most acceptable for the elderly and people with disabilities. Programs for women and the poor fell somewhere in between.[1]

This lack of clarity as to how to characterize affirmative action has affected the debate over whether affirmative action can be justified. Frequently, the affirmative action that critics attack is not the affirmative action that most people defend. For example, Carl Cohen maintains that defenders of affirmative action preferences want to award them to all the members of particular ethnic groups simply in virtue of their membership in those groups. But this view would have absurd consequences. It would mean, for example, that a minority student graduating from an inner-city high school with a fifth-grade reading ability would be an appropriate candidate for affirmative action at Harvard University. Thus, Cohen is able to win his battle against affirmative action only because he is using an absurd conception of affirmative action that no one endorses.[2]

If we are going to bring this debate any closer to a resolution, we need some agreement on what we should call affirmative action. I think it is more appropriate for critics of affirmative action to take their characterization from those who defend it rather than devise their own. Then critics of affirmative action can avoid missing their target.[3] It would also be helpful if defenders of affirmative action were to formulate their definitions so that they are acceptable to all sides. At least that is what I try to do in this book.[4]

I propose to define affirmative action as a policy of favoring qualified women, minority, or economically disadvantaged candidates over qualified men, nonminority, or economically advantaged candidates respectively with the immediate goals of outreach, remedying discrimination, or achieving diversity, and the ultimate goals of attaining a colorblind (racially just), a gender-free (sexually just), and equal opportunity (economically just) society (see diagram).[5]

Affirmative Action

Immediate goals:
- Outreach
- Remedying discrimination (Putting an end to discrimination and compensating for past discrimination).
- Diversity (To achieve certain educational or workplace benefits and to achieve equal opportunity)

Ultimate goals:
- A colorblind (racially just), gender-free (sexually just), and equal opportunity (economically just) society

---

Minorities for whom it is appropriate to pursue affirmative action are those who have been significantly harmed by past or present discrimination and/or those who can provide the benefits of diversity.[6] A colorblind and gender-free society is a society in which race and sex have no more significance than eye color has in most societies. It is a society in which the traits that are truly desirable and distributable are equally open to women and men.[7] An equal opportunity society is one where individuals with the same native abilities and skills have similar social and economic chances for developing themselves and leading a good life.

Alternatively, the ultimate goals of affirmative action can be understood to be racial justice, sexual justice and economic justice (which is a major component of an equal opportunity society).[8] Because our society is far from being racially, sexually, or economically just, it is generally recognized that to make the transition to such a society, we have to take race, sex, and economic disadvantage into account. For example, after the U.S. Civil War, Congress funded programs explicitly for the benefit of free blacks and former slaves, and after World War II, the West German government approved large compensations to individual Jews and to the newly created State of Israel.[9] In addition, the U.S. government occasionally compensates American Indians for past injustices against them. For example, in 2000, the U.S Congress approved giving a New Mexico Indian tribe $23 million and about 4,600 acres of land to settle lawsuits over land claimed under a grant from the king of Spain more than 300 years ago.[10] In 1965, Pell grants were funded for the first time in the United States, which helped disadvantaged students (primarily with family incomes of $20,000 or less) to attend post-secondary educational institutions. Initially, these grants covered 60 percent of the cost of education at a four-year institution, but today they cover only roughly one-third of the cost.[11]

Even the strongest critics of affirmative action acknowledge that to advance toward a racially and sexually just society, we will sometimes have to depart from the status quo. For example, by favoring qualified women or minority candidates over qualified men or nonminority candidates when the qualified women or minority candidates have directly suffered from proven past discrimination. Such cases are considered to be justified uses of racial or sexual classifications, and *not* as involving racial preferences. As Carl Cohen put it, "The equal protection of the laws does not forbid *every* racial classification."[12] However, these critics will typically object to any use of any kind of sexual or racial proportionality as a means for achieving a racially and sexually just society. They will regard such uses of sexual or racial proportionality to involve racial and sexual preferences and thereby to be unjust.

Other critics embrace equal opportunity affirmative action to secure a more economically just society, but at the same time reject other forms of affirmative action. These critics will favor some instances of affirmative action captured by my definition and be against other instances that are also captured by my definition. The same holds true for defenders of affirmative action. The only difference is that defenders and critics disagree about which instances of affirmative action captured by my definition we should be in favor of and which we should be against.[13]

As I define it, affirmative action can have a number of immediate goals. It can have the goal of outreach with the purpose of searching out qualified women, minority, or economically disadvantaged candidates who would otherwise not know about or apply for the available positions, but then hire or accept only those who are actually the most qualified. It can also attempt to remedy discrimination. Here there are two possibilities (see diagram above). First, an affirmative action program can be designed simply to put an end to an existing discriminatory practice, and create, possibly for the first time in a particular setting, a truly nondiscriminatory playing field. Second, it can attempt to compensate for past discrimination and its effects. The idea here is that stopping discrimination is one thing and making up for past discrimination and the effects of that discrimination is another, and that both need to be done.

Still another form of affirmative action has the goal of diversity, where the pursuit of diversity is, in turn, justified in terms of certain educational benefits it provides or its ability to legitimately create a more effective workforce in such areas as policing or community relations, or achieving equal opportunity.[14] Here it might even be said that the affirmative action candidates are, in fact, the most qualified candidates overall, because the less diverse candidates would not be as qualified.[15] As it turns out, all other forms of affirmative action can be understood in terms of their immediate goals to be outreach, remedial, or diversity. Remedial affirmative action further divides into two subtypes. One subtype seeks to end present discrimination and create a nondiscriminatory playing field and the other subtype attempts to compensate for past discrimination and its effects. Diversity affirmative action also divides into two subtypes, depending on whether it is pursued for its educational or workplace benefits or to more fully achieve equal opportunity (See Diagram).

Assuming that these are the basic types and subtypes of affirmative action, we need to examine them to determine when they can be justified. We begin with outreach affirmative action.

4

A Defense of Outreach Affirmative Action

Outreach affirmative action is easily the most defensible form of affirmative action. Even strong critics, like Louis Pojman, Thomas Sowell, and Carl Cohen defend this particular form of affirmative action. Thus, Pojman supports what he calls "weak affirmative action," which includes the "widespread advertisement to groups not previously represented in certain privileged positions." Similarly, Sowell holds that

> Racial discrimination is [an] obvious area where merely to "cease and desist" is not enough. If a firm has engaged in racial discrimination for years and has an all-white force as a result, then simply to stop explicit discrimination will mean little as long as the firm continues to hire its current employees' friends and relatives through word of mouth referrals....Clearly, the area of racial discrimination is one in which positive or affirmative steps of some kind seem reasonable.[1]

There is also considerable evidence that outreach affirmative action is needed. Social scientists have discovered that many employers tend to recruit selectively and informally, directing their efforts at neighborhoods, institutions, and media outlets that have small minority populations or constituencies.[2] For instance, in one study of Chicago area employers, it was found that in an effort to screen potential applicants, employers engaged in a variety of race-neutral recruitment mechanisms that had the effect of "disproportionately screen[ing] out inner-city blacks."[3] For example, 40 percent of employers failed to advertise job openings in newspapers and relied instead on informal employee networking to generate job applicants. Of those employers who did advertise job openings, two-thirds advertised in neighborhood or "white ethnic" newspapers rather than in "black newspapers." Although some employers recruited in both metropolitan and suburban schools, many of these employers gave applications from suburban schools more attention.[4] According to another study, about 86 percent of available jobs do not appear in classified advertisements and 80 percent of executives find their jobs through networking.[5] Thus, there is much that businesses and educational institutions can do by way of outreach affirmative action to ensure that minorities, women, and economically disadvantaged candidates know about the availability of existing jobs and positions that in the past were foreclosed to them.

In the construction industry, outreach programs sometimes require prime contractors to solicit bids and negotiate with subcontractors who are minority business enterprises (MBE) or women business enterprises (WBE) as a condition of getting a government contract. This requirement has significantly increased the participation of MBE and WBE in the construction industry. However, under California's Proposition 209 and other similar state propositions, local and state government can no longer impose this sort of requirement. Any outreach affirmative action program must be directed at other business enterprises (OBE) as well as at MBE and WBE, which can't help but dilute the outreach that was previously provided to MBE and WBE. Nevertheless, some, but not all, of that effect can be achieved in certain contexts by including a preference for local subcontractors.

Summing up the main requirement for outreach affirmative action is the following:

> All reasonable steps must be taken to ensure that qualified minority, women, and economically disadvantaged candidates are made as aware of existing jobs and positions that are available to them as are nonminority, male, or economically advantaged candidates.

5

A Defense of Remedial Affirmative Action

Compensating for Past Discrimination

Although the U.S. Supreme Court has adopted different positions at different times, it has always held that it is permissible to adopt remedial affirmative action as compensation for identifiable acts of purposeful discrimination committed by that very institution. Of course, it is rare for an institution that is engaging in affirmative action to actually admit that it has committed identifiable acts of purposeful discrimination, or that it did so in the recent past. This is because such an admission would render the institution vulnerable to claims of compensation from other victims. Consequently, institutions frequently engage in remedial affirmative action only when they have been found guilty of discrimination, or, more likely, when they have been "forced" to accept a legal settlement.

In 1973, AT&T reached a settlement with the Justice Department in which it agreed to restructure its hiring and promotion policies. Until then, half the company's 700,000 employees were women, all of whom were either telephone operators or secretaries. The company had been categorizing virtually all of its jobs as either men's work or women's work. Women, along with minority men, were virtually excluded from the higher paying positions in the company.[1] The agreement resulted in $15 million in back wages to 13,000 women and 2,000 minority men, and $23 million in raises to 36,000 employees who had been harmed by previous policies.[2]

In 1993, Shoney's Restaurant chain settled a racial discrimination case against it.[3] Shoney's had been tracking blacks into kitchen jobs so that most employees in the dining area would be white. The case arose when two white managers complained that they had been pressured by their supervisors to restrict blacks to kitchen jobs, and that they had been fired when they had resisted that pressure. As more evidence was gathered, the case grew into a nationwide class-action suit against Shoney's.[4] The case was settled out of court for $105 million.[5]

In 1997, Texaco reached a settlement in a class-action suit against it charging that the company systematically passed over black employees for promotions in favor of less experienced whites, and that the company fostered a racially hostile environment.[6] Some participants in the suit contended that they were called "uppity" for asking questions; others said that black employees were called "orangutans" and "porch monkeys."[7] The agreement was reached after the disclosure of a secret tape recording of senior Texaco executives, revealing them planning the destruction of documents demanded in the lawsuit and belittling black employees, referring to them as "black jelly beans" and "niggers."[8] The settlement for $176 million is the largest race-discrimination settlement in U.S. history.[9] It called for lump sum payments averaging around $63,000 to about 1,300 black employees.[10] In addition, salaried blacks still working for Texaco received an 11 percent pay raise worth an estimated $26 million over five years. Texaco also paid $35 million for a five-year task force that revised its personnel programs.[11] Peter Bijur, who was chair and CEO of Texaco at the time, said that the racial discrimination problems at his company represented just the "tip of the iceberg" in corporate America.[12]

In 2000, the Coca-Cola Company agreed to settle a racial discrimination case in which it was accused of erecting a corporate hierarchy where black employees were clustered at the bottom of the pay scale, averaging $26,000 a year less than white workers.[13] One plaintiff, who worked for Coca-Cola for thirteen years, said she made less than white workers she supervised.

The settlement of $156 million provided as many as 2,000 current and former black salaried employees with an average of $40,000, while the four main plaintiffs received up to $300,000 apiece.[14]

Ending Present Discrimination

Since in all four cases compensation was paid to those who claimed they were harmed by the discriminatory practices of their companies, few opponents of affirmative action have objected to these remedial actions. However, there are other forms of remedial affirmative action in which the individuals who benefit are not the ones who were actually discriminated against by the institution that is providing the remedial affirmative action.[15] For instance, in *Local 28 Sheet Metal Workers' International v. EEOC* (1986), the U.S. Supreme Court upheld a remedial affirmative action program that required Local 28 in New York City to increase its minority membership by admitting into its training program one minority apprentice for each nonminority apprentice until the union reached a 29 percent minority membership.[16] This percentage was based on the number of minorities in the relevant labor pool in New York City at the time. From 1964 to 1986, Local 28 had been found in contempt of every legal attempt to get it to admit minorities into its virtually all-white union. In fact, in 1966 minority applicants, benefiting from a tutoring program, were awarded nine of the top ten scores and 75 percent of the top sixty-five scores on the union's own apprenticeship test, but the union refused to abide by the results of its own test.[17]

Clearly, the main beneficiaries of the Court's decision were to be minorities subsequently admitted into the union by way of its apprenticeship program; these beneficiaries would not be, for the most part, persons who had been previously discriminated against by the union. Thus, there is no reason to think that those who would benefit, once the union stopped discriminating, would be limited to persons against whom the union had actually discriminated. Rather, they would be minorities who, under conditions of equal opportunity, would be admitted into the union roughly in proportion to their availability in the relevant labor pool.[18] The Supreme Court's decision should be viewed as an attempt to create an equal opportunity playing field from which minorities would rightly benefit, even if they hadn't been harmed by Local 28's past discriminatory practices.[19] Yet sometimes remedial affirmative action will attempt to do more than simply create an equal opportunity playing field. It will also attempt to correct for the harm done by present and past discrimination, as the AT&T, Shoney's, Texaco, and Coca-Cola cases demonstrate.

Statistical Disparities

In making the case for remedial affirmative action, it is generally useful to be able to appeal to statistical disparities (disparate impact) as prima facie evidence of a discriminatory practice. The fact that 50 percent of AT&T's work force during the late 1960s and early 1970s were women, at the same time that they were almost totally absent from management or craft worker positions, was assumed to be prima facie evidence that AT&T had discriminated against them.[20] Similarly, the fact that there were virtually no minority members in New York City's Local 28, when minorities made up 29 percent of the relevant labor pool, was assumed to be prima facie evidence that Local 28 was discriminating against minorities.[21] Of course, it is always possible that such prima facie evidence of discrimination can be rebutted, but it is important, once such evidence has been provided, that the burden of proof should shift to the employer or union to show why this disparity was unavoidable.

There is also good reason to think that the use of statistical disparities (disparate impacts) to establish a prima facie case for discrimination should be more broadly applied throughout society. Thus, Barbara Bergman has shown that if you look at U.S. industry by occupational sectors, there is considerable variation among businesses within each section with respect to their utilization of women and minorities.[22] For example, within the auto industry, General Motors has three times as many women managers as Ford, and among retail businesses, McDonald's has four times as many minority managers as Safeway Stores and twice as many as Kroger.[23] Disparities such as these need to be further investigated to determine whether or not they might provide grounds for remedial affirmative action.

It is sometimes objected that statistical disparities do not provide suitable grounds for claims of discrimination. Thomas Sowell has argued that discrimination alone cannot explain the presence or absence of statistical disparities between different ethnic groups.[24] Sowell points out that groups such as the Japanese and Chinese Americans have fared very well despite racial discrimination against them.[25] But while Sowell is right that an *absence* of statistical disparities may be due to the fact that racial discrimination has been overcome with respect to some groups (e.g., Japanese and Chinese Americans), this does not prove that the *presence* of disparities with respect to other groups in the United States (e.g., African Americans, American Indians, Hispanic Americans, and even other subgroups of Asian Americans, such as Laotian and Filipino Americans) is not due to more virulent forms of racial discrimination that have yet to be overcome. Nor does it show that a government committed to both equal opportunity and rectifying for past discrimination would not want to correct these more virulent forms of discrimination with remedial affirmative action. In fact, such utilization of statistical disparities has been endorsed by the U.S Supreme Court:

> There is no doubt that where gross statistical disparities can be shown, they alone in a proper case may constitute prima facie proof of a pattern or practice of discrimination.[26]

Actually, all that is being claimed about statistical disparities is that when they occur, it is necessary to check to see if they have resulted from discrimination. When Sowell claims that there is "a very large body of history about groups who began in lowly positions and then rose to levels above the average member of the larger society" and that "Jewish, Chinese, Lebanese, Indian, Japanese, German, Italian and other immigrants have done this around the world,"[27] he has already gone beyond merely noting the statistical disparity in one country. He shows that the disparity occurs around the world and, in some cases, those who are now prosperous started out in lowly positions, where presumably they could not have discriminated against anyone. Providing such further evidence that shows that the original statistical disparity is not the product of discrimination is all that the defender of remedial affirmative action wants and that is just what Sowell concedes is needed.[28]

There is good reason, therefore, to recognize that statistical disparities can serve a prima facie evidence of discrimination, which then must be shown to be operationally necessary for the business, union, or institution involved in order to preclude the need for remedial affirmative action.[29]

Restrictions by the U.S. Supreme Court

Despite its recognition of the relevance of statistical disparities to determine that discrimination has occurred, the Supreme Court has restricted the use of such disparities in justifying remedial affirmative action programs. Consider the decision the U.S. Supreme Court reached in *Croson* (1989). The Court held that a generalized assertion of past discrimination in the entire construction industry (the basis of the federal set-aside accepted in *Fullilove* 1980) was insufficient to justify a minority set-aside by the city of Richmond. The Court also ruled that further evidence showing that the population of Richmond was 50 percent black while less than 1 percent of the city's construction business had been awarded to minority-owned enterprises, and that all the building trade associations in Virginia had at most one or two black members, was insufficient to justify the city's affirmative action program. The Court further held that the relevant comparison in this case was not between the percentage of blacks in Richmond and the percentage of the city's construction business that had been awarded to minority-owned enterprises, but rather the comparison between the number of minority-owned enterprises in Richmond and the percentage of the city's construction business that had been awarded to minority-owned enterprises. The Court's general view was that when special qualifications are required to fill particular jobs, the relevant comparison is not to the general population, but rather to the smaller group of individuals who possess the necessary qualifications. But if discrimination was as rampant in the construction industry nationwide, as in the city of Richmond, clearly not many minority-owned enterprises would have been able to survive in that environment. Thus a small number of minority-owned enterprises in the Richmond area are exactly what one would expect if there had been significant discrimination. Accordingly, we should not be able to use the existence of a small number of minority-owned enterprises to indicate the absence of discrimination. In fact, without an explanation to the contrary, it would be reasonable to infer that a small number of minority-owned enterprises in the Richmond area are, in fact, evidence of discrimination. Why else would minorities in the Richmond area not have taken advantage of the construction opportunities present, if those opportunities had in fact been open to them? In the South, under slavery, more than 80 percent of those working as masons, blacksmiths, carpenters, and painters were slaves, according to a census taken in 1865.[30] Even in the case at issue, Croson, the owner of the white-owned, Ohio-based enterprise, actually lost his contract with the city of Richmond because Brown, the owner of the minority-owned, Richmond-based firm that Croson tried to subcontract, astutely took advantage of the opportunity provided to bypass Croson and to deal directly with the city.

In addition to the U.S. Supreme Court's overly restrictive standard for proof of discrimination, the Court requires that any institution that seeks to compensate for past discrimination must itself be guilty of that very discrimination. In the *Croson case,* the Court ruled against the city of Richmond because the city did not sufficiently implicate itself in the past discrimination that it sought to correct. But most institutions that are considering whether to engage in remedial affirmative action would understandably be reluctant to implicate themselves in the very discrimination they are seeking to correct because that would, in turn, open them up to liability and censure. Moreover, once sufficient evidence of discrimination has been provided, there seems to be no reason to impose the additional requirement that the agent engaged in the affirmative action program must also be implicated in the discrimination it is seeking to correct. This is the overly restrictive position the Supreme Court has endorsed, making it very difficult to have a court-sanctioned remedial affirmative action program.

Benign and Invidious Racial Classifications

The U.S. Supreme Court assumes that racial classifications are presumptively suspect.[31] It seems to take that assumption to imply that it does not matter whether the classifications are intended to remedy the results of past discrimination or intended to foster or maintain that discrimination; the Court regards both uses of racial classification as equally suspect. As the Court put it in *Adarand Constructors v. Pena* (1995), quoting the *Croson* decision (1986):

> Absent searching judicial inquiry into the justification for such race-based measures, there is simply no way of determining what classifications are "benign" or "remedial," and what classifications are in fact motivated by

illegitimate notions of racial inferiority or simple racial politics. Indeed, the purpose of strict scrutiny is to "smoke out" illegitimate uses of race by assuring that the legislative body is pursuing a goal important enough to warrant use of a highly suspect tool. The test also ensures that the means chosen "fit" this compelling goal so closely that there is little or no possibility that the motive for the classification was illegitimate racial prejudice or stereotype.

In his dissent in *Adarand,* Justice Stevens interprets the majority as claiming that it is difficult to distinguish between benign or remedial uses of racial classifications, on the one hand, and that invidious discrimination, which was so characteristic of the U.S. racist past, on the other. By contrast, as Stevens graphically puts it, the distinction that needs to be made is between a welcome mat and a "No Trespassing" sign, and this distinction, Stevens argues, is one we not only can, but do make fairly easily, with respect to the motives and the consequences of these two uses of racial classifications.

Consider some of the motives underlying traditional racial discrimination in the United States. Blacks were not hired or admitted into schools because it was thought that contact with them was degrading and contaminating to whites. These policies were based on contempt and loathing for blacks, on a belief that blacks were less than fully developed human beings suitable only for subordinate positions in society. By contrast, under remedial affirmative action, whites are not being passed over for any of these reasons. No defender of affirmative action thinks that contact with whites is degrading or contaminating, that whites are contemptible and loathsome, or that whites, by their nature, should be subordinate to blacks. Similarly, the consequences of these two uses of racial classifications are radically different. Affirmative action does not stigmatize whites, it does not perpetuate negative stereotypes about them; it is not part of a pattern of discrimination that makes being white extremely burdensome. Nor does it increase an already dominant group's supply of power, authority, opportunity, and wealth, as did traditional racial discrimination. On the contrary, it results in a more egalitarian distribution of social and economic goods.[32]

Yet while Justice Stevens is right in that we can easily distinguish between paradigm cases of benign and invidious racial classifications, the majority of the Court in *Adarand* may not be denying that this is the case. Instead, the Court may be worried that those who are advancing so-called benign and remedial uses of racial classifications may have less than ideal motives. For example, instead of being motivated to rectify for past injustices and to give minorities what they deserve, those favoring remedial affirmative action may believe that minorities are naturally inferior and so need special help (the racial paternalism that Justice Thomas seems to fear). Or, more likely, they may simply be trying to secure a special advantage for minorities without justifying it as a remedy for past wrongs. No doubt we should not want to approve of affirmative action programs that are driven by these less worthy motives. But no evidence of such motives has been provided in the affirmative action cases that have come before the Supreme Court. All the evidence in the *Croson* case, for example, pointed to significant past discrimination in the construction industry in the city of Richmond. This should have been sufficient evidence to support a remedial affirmative action program, even assuming that all racial classifications are presumptively suspect. Unfortunately, the Supreme Court in its recent decisions has imposed unnecessary and irrelevant requirements on what counts as proof of past discrimination thus making it extremely difficult to effect such remedies.

From its assumption that racial classifications are presumptively suspect, the Supreme Court infers the need for a strict scrutiny analysis, which means that it must be possible to show that the use of a racial classification is narrowly tailored to meet a compelling government interest. Given that ending racial discrimination and eliminating the burdensome effects of past discrimination are clearly compelling (government) interests, everything turns on how narrowly tailored the affirmative action program has to be in serving those interests. And here too the U.S. Supreme Court and some lower courts have been unreasonably demanding.[33]

Consider again the *Croson* decision. Richmond's affirmative action plan specified the minorities who could benefit from its plan as "citizens of the United States who are Blacks, Spanish-speaking, Oriental, Indians, Eskimos or Aleuts," using the same specification of minorities that Congress had employed in fashioning its affirmative action set-aside program on which the Richmond program was patterned. Now it is arguable whether this part of the plan is narrowly tailored, as no evidence was given for including Spanish-speaking, Orientals, Indians, Eskimos, or Aleuts in the Richmond affirmative action program. Nevertheless, it could have been argued that opening up the construction industry in Richmond to members of these groups would also serve to break down discrimination against African Americans. Yet, even accepting the majority's view that Richmond's ordinance was overbroad, it does not follow that this should invalidate Richmond's ordinance as a whole. After all, as this affirmative action program functioned in the city of Richmond, only African American contractors actually benefited from it.

Racial Discrimination versus Sexual Discrimination

It is important to recognize that the U.S. Supreme Court does not demand the same standard of proof in dealing with sexual discrimination that it does for racial discrimination. Despite the widespread evidence of sexual discrimination, the Supreme Court has advanced a number of arguments for treating it differently than racial discrimination. In *Bakke* (1978), Justice Powell argued that in the case of sexual discrimination, there is just one oppressed group (women) and just one oppressor group (men) making it easier to determine what sort of remedies are appropriate. By contrast, in the case of racial oppression, there are rival groups that can claim that they are oppressed, and the groups that can reasonably make this claim vary over time, so the argument for remedying racial discrimination must be made on a case-by-case basis. However, the same holds true for sexual discrimination; the argument for rectifying sexual discrimination must also be made case by case. The courts have not accepted, nor should they accept, the argument that women have generally been discriminated against by men and are generally entitled to remedial affirmative action. For example, it is unlikely that women employed in the nursing profession today deserve remedial affirmative action. But there are other areas, like the construction industry, in which remedial affirmative action would be appropriate for women. The argument for remedial affirmative action for women therefore has to be made on a case-by-case basis, just as the argument for remedial affirmative action for minorities has to be made on a case-by-case basis. There is no difference in this regard.

The U.S. Supreme Court has also argued that racial discrimination is a more invidious harm than sexual discrimination, and for this reason we should require a more restrictive standard of proof for using racial classifications. Now it is no more useful to try to rank the evils of racism and sexism in our society than it is to try to rank the evils of black slavery and the Holocaust.[34] Even if we assume, for the sake of argument, that racial discrimination is more invidious than sexual discrimination, by imposing a more restrictive standard of proof with respect to the use of racial classifications, the Supreme Court makes it more difficult to correct for racial discrimination than to correct for sexual discrimination. But this is just the opposite of what the Court should be doing under its assumption that racial discrimination is more invidious than sexual discrimination. What this means is that the Supreme Court's standard of proof of racial discrimination, especially given the Court's view that racial discriminations is more invidious than sexual discrimination, should be no more restrictive than its standard for sexual discrimination. This would allow race- and sex-based remedial affirmative action to be similarly justified when reasonably related to the justifiable state purpose of ending and compensating for discrimination against women and minorities in U.S. society.

A Better Standard of Proof for Remedial Affirmative Action

Assuming that the standard of proof for remedial affirmative action for minorities were so modified, it would then be far easier to use race-based affirmative action to correct and compensate for widespread discriminatory practices in U.S. society. For example, it is generally recognized that in many parts of the United States there are de facto segregated primary and secondary educational systems whose existence is clearly rooted in past discrimination. In fact, U.S. primary and secondary schools are now becoming even more segregated than they were in the past.[35] In the South—the most integrated region of the country—the percentage of black students in predominantly white schools fell from a peak of 43.5 percent in the late 1980s to 34.7 percent in 1996, even falling below the level achieved twenty-four years earlier in 1972.

National trends in the United States parallel those in the South. Nationwide, the percentage of black students in majority white schools peaked in the early 1980s but then declined to the levels of the 1960s. The percentage of Hispanics in majority white schools has declined from 45 percent in 1968 to 25 percent today. Both in terms of resources and race, U.S. schools have become at least as segregated as they were in the 1960s. In large cities, fifteen of every sixteen black and Hispanic students are in schools where most of the students are nonwhite. In medium-size cities, the statistics are 63 percent of blacks and 70 percent of Hispanics. White suburban schools have approximately twice the funds per student compared to urban schools where black and Hispanic students are concentrated, although people living in urban school districts are taxed more heavily to support their poorer schools.

Much of this racial segregation in primary and secondary schools in the United States can be traced to the widespread discrimination in housing. In 1939, the Federal Housing Authority's (FHA) guidelines for granting housing loans explicitly used race as the single most important criterion: "If a neighborhood is to retain stability, it is necessary that properties shall be continued to be occupied by the same social and racial classes." The FHA further created segregation in the suburban areas by recommending that "developers place [racially restrictive] covenants on all housing that they built to ensure its future worth." A bias in favor of the suburbs was also evident in FHA practices and regulations, which favored the construction of single-family homes. In addition, the FHA made it easier and cheaper for a family to purchase a new home than to renovate an older one.[36] As a result, the vast majority of FHA and Veteran's Administration (VA) mortgages went to white middle-class suburbs; very few were awarded to black neighborhoods in central cities. For example, FHA lending per capita in the New York City suburb of Nassau County (Long Island) was eleven times that of Kings County (Brooklyn) and sixty times that of Bronx County (the Bronx). By the late 1950s many inner cities were locked into a spiral of decline that was both encouraged and supported by federal housing policies.

During the 1950s and 1960s local authorities were also encouraged and supported by the federal government to carry out widespread slum clearance in growing black neighborhoods that threatened white business districts and elite institutions. Public housing was used to house black families displaced by the razing of neighborhoods undergoing renewal. Multiunit projects of extremely high density were built to house as many blacks as possible. Because of these federal policies and programs, blacks and minorities in the United States actually became more separated and isolated than they ever had been before.[37] Congress specifically excluded federal mortgage insurance from coverage under the Civil Rights Act of 1964 to allow the widespread discrimination in the FHA and VA loan programs to continue.

Following the 1968 assassination of Martin Luther King, Jr., and the accompanying urban riots, however, Congress passed the Fair Housing Act, which banned discrimination in the sale or rental of housing. Unfortunately, as the price for its enactment, its enforcement provisions were systematically gutted. Under the Act, the Department of Housing and Urban Development (HUD) was only authorized to investigate complaints of housing discrimination made by "aggrieved persons," and if HUD chose to pursue a complaint, it was only empowered to engage in "conciliation" to resolve the problem. According to one study, only 20 to 30 percent of complaints that were filed reached formal mediation, and nearly half of them remained in noncompliance after conciliation efforts had been terminated. Because HUD had no power of enforcement, the act's main enforcement mechanism was private suits, but these suits were limited to only actual damages and a $1,000 punitive award. In addition, the Act held plaintiffs specifically liable for all court costs and attorney fees unless they were unable to pay for them. In practice the Fair Housing Act of 1968 allowed a few victims to gain redress, while permitting an extensive system of institutionalized discrimination to remain in place. That is why only about 400 fair housing cases have been decided since 1968, compared with more than 2 million incidents of housing discrimination that are estimated to occur each year.

Twenty years later, over stiff opposition from President Reagan, Congress passed the Fair Housing Amendments Act of 1988, which extended the time to file a housing discrimination complaint, allowed attorney fees and court costs to be recovered by prevailing plaintiffs, and increased the punitive awards to $10,000 for first and second offenses, $50,000 for a third offense. Unfortunately, the amended act continued to rely heavily on individuals who are willing to sue, the so-called private attorney generals, rather than on federal authorities.[38] Consequently, the high level of segregation found in U.S. cities has hardly changed since the passage of the Fair Housing Act of 1968.[39]

The widespread discrimination in housing has an enormous impact on the quality of K through 12 education because the primary funding for such schools is derived from local property taxes on the homes in each school district; the more expensive the homes in a particular district, the more local property tax money is available for support of the schools in that district. The United States happens to be unique among advanced nations in making primary and secondary education so strongly dependent on the wealth of the families in corresponding school districts.[40] Unfortunately, the concentrating of whites and minorities in school districts with significantly different economic resources allows discrimination in housing to transmute into discrimination in K through 12 schooling.

Ideally, such educational disparity should be corrected with an equal education opportunity program that, within a short period of time, would provide every child in the United States with equally good educational opportunities, kindergarten through twelfth grade, for, let's say, the additional cost of $25 billion a year of federal and state support of local school districts. Moreover, if we had to choose between existing affirmative action programs and such an equal education opportunity program—if we could not have them both—then there would be no question among defenders of affirmative action as to which one to choose.[41] Of course, in the real world in which we live, we do not currently have the option of having the proposed equal education opportunity program. This alternative to maintaining and developing existing affirmative action programs is simply not a feasible option, at present, at least not in the United States.

What then should we do? Consider the following statistical amalgam of a typical recent African American high school graduate. Let's call him Daryl Williams and imagine him considering whether or not to attend college. We can expect that Daryl's family wealth and income, parents' education, the high school he attended, and the neighborhood he lives in are not strongly correlated with Daryl's attending college, certainly not with his attending an elite college. Daryl's parents have most likely experienced various forms of racial discrimination in the workplace, in housing, in acquiring loans. The high school Daryl attended probably had fewer teachers who were experienced and credentialed in the subjects they were teaching and fewer, if any, AP courses than the high schools typically attended by whites. All of these factors impact on the extent to which Daryl was counseled and prepared for attending college, certainly with whether he was counseling and prepared for attending an elite college or university.

Daryl also probably had more encounters with the police, and surely more serious encounters with the law, than a typical white high school student who had engaged in similar behavior. This is because African Americans, compared to similarly situated whites, are more likely to be stopped by the police, searched when stopped, arrested, booked on felony charges, refused a low bail, tried, convicted, denied probation, denied an alternative sentence, sentenced to prison, and denied parole.[42] If Daryl had looked for a summer or part-time job, he was also less likely to be offered employment than similarly qualified, or even less qualified, whites. As noted before, employers actually prefer to hire white ex-cons over equally qualified black applicants who have no criminal record.

In light of what we know about Daryl, our typical African American high school student, what then should we do? Recognizing that the lesser credentials that minorities have in the United States today are often the result of present or past discriminatory practices, both institutions of higher education and employers could use affirmative action programs to make up for that discrimination. These affirmative action programs would favor qualified minority candidates who have been discriminated against in the past or present over equally or more qualified nonminority candidates who have not been similarly disadvantaged. In fact, it should be the case that those who are passed over by such programs have themselves benefited from the discrimination suffered by these affirmative action candidates, for example, the discrimination found in their unequal educational and residential opportunities.[43] Yet, to be justified, such affirmative action programs must favor only candidates whose qualifications are such that when their selection is combined with a suitably designed educational enhancement program, they will normally turn out, within a reasonably short time, to be as qualified as, or even more qualified than, their peers. Such candidates must have the potential to be as qualified as, or more qualified than, their peers, although that potential will not yet have been actualized because of past or present discrimination. Affirmative action of this sort, with its suitably designed educational enhancement program, purports to actualize such potential.[44] In this way, persons who receive this form of affirmative action are like runners in a race who are forced to compete at a disadvantage with the other runners, say, by having weights tied to their legs, but later are allowed to remove the weights and receive special assistance for an appropriate period of time, so that the results of the race will turn out to be fair. Affirmative action of this sort, therefore, is a policy that is directed at only those minority candidates who are highly qualified, yet, because of past or present discrimination and prejudice, are less qualified than they would otherwise be. It seeks to provide such candidates with a benefit that will nullify the effects of past and present injustices by enabling them to become as qualified as, or more qualified than, their peers. Thus, once the standards of proof for race-based remedial affirmative action are rendered no more restrictive than those that are used for sex-based remedial affirmative action, so that it is just as easy to correct for the one form of discrimination as to correct for the other, it should then be possible to remedy a broad range of present and past race-based discriminatory practices.

To sum up, the requirements as to when remedial affirmative action is justified should be as follows:

1) The past discrimination that is to be remedied must be proven discrimination, but the institution that is engaging in the affirmative action need not be implicated in that proven discrimination in order for the affirmative action in question to be justified.

2) Although, in a colorblind (racially just) society, racial classifications would no longer be presumptively suspect, in the United States, they must be regarded as such because of the 250 years of slavery, 100 years of Jim Crow laws, plus discriminatory practices that continue right up to the present day. However, the standard of proof required to justify the use of racial classifications in remedial affirmative action should not be unreasonably high as it was in the *Croson* case. It should not be easier to correct sexual discrimination in society than it is to correct racial discrimination. Accordingly, remedial affirmative action still has a significant role in combating proven past and present discrimination in housing, education, and jobs, unless more broadly conceived and much better funded corrective policies to more directly remedy these injustices are undertaken.

3) Only those candidates would be selected whose qualifications are such that when their selection is combined with a suitably designed educational enhancement program, they will normally turn out, within a reasonably short time, to be as qualified as, or even more qualified than, their peers.

4) Those who are passed over by such affirmative action programs would have themselves been found to have benefited from the discrimination suffered by the affirmative action candidates, for example, the discrimination found in their unequal educational and residential opportunities.[45]

6

Objections to Remedial
Affirmative Action

The remedial affirmative action that I have defended in the previous chapter has been criticized in various ways. Specifically, critics have claimed that it is objectionable for the following reasons:

1) It is not required to compensate for unjust institutions of the distant past.
2) It confuses the legitimate goal of eliminating discrimination with the illegitimate one of seeking certain proportionate outcomes.
3) It requires group rights that are immoral.
4) It is directed at the wrong people.
5) It is illegal and unconstitutional.

Let me consider each of these objections in turn.

First Objection

With respect to the first objection that affirmative action is not required by the existence of unjust institutions in the past such as slavery in the

United States, Christopher Morris argues that compensation for past injustices is owed only to individuals who would have been better off except for those past injustices.[1] Individual African Americans living today, he argues, would not have been better off if there had been no slavery, because, given the contingencies of procreation, most of them would not even have been born if their ancestors had not been forcibly uprooted from Africa, enslaved, and brought to this country. Of course, in the absence of slavery and the racism it engendered, some Africans would surely have emigrated to the United States. But they would have done so more like other immigrants, and their contemporary descendants would be different individuals from most present-day African Americans who trace their history through the practice of slavery.

I think the best response to this objection is not to deny that most African Americans today are the product of slavery and would not have existed without it. Rather, the response should be to maintain that this fact by itself does not show that present-day African Americans have not been harmed by those injustices of the distant past as well as injustices of more recent vintage.[2]

To see why this is the case, consider an owner of an industrial plant arguing that she really did not harm your daughter who is suffering from leukemia due to the contaminants that leaked into the area surrounding the plant because the plant would not have opened up, nor would you have moved nearby to work, nor would this daughter of yours even been born, without its operating in this profitable way.[3] In brief, the owner of the plant contends that your daughter was not really harmed at all because, if there had been no contamination, she would not even have been born. Assuming, however, that we reject the plant owner's counterfactual requirement for harming in favor of a direct causal one (the operation of the plant caused your daughter's leukemia), as we should, then, we have to recognize that present-day African Americans would still have been harmed by the past injustices of American slavery, even though they, without the practice of slavery in the United States, like your daughter in the hypothetical example, would not have been born.

In addition, there are more recent injustices to African Americans—segregated housing, unequal education, job discrimination, inadequate health and welfare programs—all of which African Americans today would certainly be better off without. Of course, these current injustices have their origins in the injustices of the past, particularly in the institutions of slavery in the United States and the Jim Crow laws that succeeded it. However, the grounds that present-day African Americans can claim for compensation need not rest simply on the injustices of the distant past, but also on the ongoing injustices that make them worse off as individuals—injustices that other contemporary Americans are responsible for and could do something about, in part by endorsing affirmative action programs.

Second Objection

In support of the second objection that remedial affirmative action confuses the legitimate goal of eliminating discrimination with the illegitimate one of seeking certain proportionate outcomes, Carl Cohen, Terry Eastland, Thomas Sowell, and others have distinguished between a good form of affirmative action that aims at eliminating racial and sexual discrimination, which they accept, and a bad form of affirmative action that seeks certain proportionate outcomes based on race or sex, which they reject. The good form of affirmative action is further associated with the Equal Protection Clause of the Fourteenth Amendment, the Civil Rights Act of 1964, and certain Supreme Court decisions. The bad form of affirmative action is associated with certain bureaucratic decisions of the federal government and other Supreme Court decisions that are regarded as objectionable. According to Cohen:

> In its original sense, affirmative action was intended to insure the elimination of racially discriminatory practices—that is the sense in which the phrase is used in the Civil Rights Act of 1964.... But if by affirmative action one means (as most Americans now do mean) preferential devices to bring about redistribution of the good things of life to match ethnic proportions in population, affirmative action in this sense must be rejected.[4]

But are these two forms of affirmative action really that distinct? Suppose we want to engage in the first form of affirmative action, that is, we want to eliminate racially and sexually discriminatory practices. How do we go about it? If we are faced with overt, clearly documented cases of discrimination, our task is comparatively easy. If the law prohibits discrimination, it is fairly easy, for example, to remove the "Whites Only" signs. However, at least since the Civil Rights Act of 1964, discrimination in the

United States has become less overt and is more likely to be expressed in disparate treatment, as evidenced by the data and studies cited earlier. For example, in 1973, it was quite helpful to draw attention to the fact that, while half of AT&T's 700,000 employees were women, all of them were either telephone operators or secretaries, and in 1993, it was quite helpful to draw attention to the fact that most of the blacks employed by Shoney's Restaurant chain worked in the kitchen. This is why the Supreme Court has held that

> There is no doubt that where gross statistical disparities can be shown, they alone in a proper case may constitute prima facie proof of a pattern or practice of discrimination.[5]

However, when we attempt to correct for such disparities because we have determined them to be discriminatory, we bring about a more reasonable proportionate outcome, with, for example, more women employed in more of the high-paying jobs at AT&T, and more blacks employed outside the kitchen in Shoney's Restaurants. This shows that when we engage in the first form of affirmative action, and thus attempt to eliminate discrimination, we will be led to pay attention to gross statistical disparities effecting minorities or women, and that when we find that these statistical disparities cannot be justified, we will be led to replace them with a reasonable proportionate outcome for the relevant minorities and women. This also shows that when we engage in the first form of affirmative action, we will be led, naturally and justifiably, to engage in the second form of affirmative action, and that those who endorse the first form of affirmative action, as many do, cannot consistently avoid endorsing the second as well.

Third Objection

In support of the third objection that affirmative action requires group rights that are immoral, Carl Cohen claims,

> Moral entitlements are not held by groups. Whites as a group do not have rights; blacks as a group do not have rights. Rights are possessed by persons. As when persons are entitled to be made whole for some injury earlier done

to them, the duty owed is not to members of their race or sex or nationality, not to their group, but to them as individuals. The effort to defend preference as group compensation fails because it fundamentally misconceives the relation between wrongs and remedies.[6]

But groups can and do have moral entitlements.[7] For example, in most countries, political parties are morally and legally entitled to use the monetary contributions of their members for various purposes. Moreover, any moral entitlement an individual possesses is shared by some group or other, that is, it is held in virtue of some feature that the individual shares with the members of a particular group. For example, if a high school student deserves to be admitted to some prestigious college, it is in virtue of excellences the student shares with a group of students who also deserve to be admitted.

Nor is the defender of remedial affirmative action committed to compensating anyone simply because he or she happens to be a member of a particular racial group or simply to achieve a racial proportionalism, as Cohen claims. To do so would actually involve violating the thesis made famous by the Scottish philosopher David Hume—you cannot derive an "ought" from an "is." In this context, the violation would involve attempting deriving an ought-statement—that one ought to receive remedial affirmative action, from an is-statement—that one is a member of a certain racial group or because it achieves a racial proportionalism, a derivation, which, according to Hume's thesis, cannot be made.

Not surprisingly, a defense of remedial affirmative action is perfectly compatible with Hume's thesis. Such a defense does not require a move from "is" to "ought." Rather, the justification of remedial affirmative action proceeds by way of deriving an "ought" in a logically appropriate way from other "oughts."

For example, let's take the Supreme Court decision in *Local 28 of the Sheet Metal Workers' International v. EEOC* (1986). New York City's Local 28 had been found in contempt of every legal attempt to get it to admit minorities into its virtually all-white union from 1964 to 1986. To put a stop to that discrimination, the Supreme Court imposed a racial proportionality. It required Local 28 to increase its minority membership by admitting one minority apprentice for each nonminority apprentice until the union reached a 29 percent minority membership. This percentage was based on the number of minorities in the relevant labor pool in New York City at the time. The argument of the Court can be expressed as follows:

1) The racial discrimination of Local 28 ought to be stopped.
2) The proposed racial proportionality is an appropriate means for stopping that discrimination.
3) An affirmative action program employing the proposed racial proportionality ought to be implemented.

Clearly, this argument moves from an "ought" to an "ought," and so it does not violate Hume's thesis.

An argument with a similar structure can be used to support the settlement in the Shoney's Restaurant chain case (see chapter 5). To put an end to discrimination and to compensate for past discrimination, minority employees were given a financial settlement and moved out of the kitchen and into the dining area.[8]

Even in particular contexts where all blacks deserve remedial affirmative action because of current discriminatory practices or past discrimination and the effects thereof, they do not deserve it because they are black, or because they belong to the group of black individuals. Rather, they deserve it because, in the particular contexts, it puts an end to discriminatory practices or compensates those who have been discriminated against or those who suffer from the effects of past discrimination. Thus, the racial predicate (being a member of a particular racial group) is linked to a nonracial predicate (e.g., benefiting from putting an end to a discriminatory practice or compensated for actually suffering from past discrimination in a particular context) with the goal of suitably constituting an "ought" premise from which a remedial affirmative action "ought" conclusion can be derived.[9] Of course, we can always debate whether particular instances of this form of argument are justified.[10] Yet what is perfectly clear is that defenders of affirmative action need not be attempting to derive an "ought" from an "is."

What this shows is that both the defenders of affirmative action and its critics agree that the only appropriate grounds for claiming that an individual deserves remedial affirmative action is that the person himself or herself is benefiting from putting an end to a discriminatory practice or has actually suffered discrimination or the effects thereof. Where defenders and critics disagree, however, is over when those grounds are satisfied.

Suppose an elite university wanted to employ a remedial affirmative action policy to admit minorities from segregated, underfunded inner-city schools with somewhat lower grades and SAT scores than whites from surrounding well-funded suburban districts. Taking into account the current practices of discrimination (see chapter 1) and discriminatory practices that gave rise to the segregated housing and school districting (see chapter 5), why would this not provide sufficient grounds, other things being equal, for a remedial affirmative action program that admitted such students? Suppose one also did a comparative evaluation of all the applicants to the university to ensure that all other things were equal. Why then would this not suffice to justify such a remedial affirmative action program?

Let's consider an analogous comparative evaluation that elite colleges and universities actually do make. Such colleges and universities presumably want to ensure that they admit those applicants who are most qualified to benefit from the educational experience they provide and most likely to make important contributions to the educational development of their peers and to society more generally. Similarly, elite professional schools want to ensure that they admit those applicants who are most qualified to become talented and responsible lawyers, doctors, engineers, accountants, and so on. Nevertheless, to implement these goals, U.S. colleges and universities have generally relied on grades and standardized tests that they recognize do not correlate at all with the goals they endorse.

SAT scores, for example, only correlate 18 percent with first-year grades, and are even less predictive in subsequent years. LSAT scores at the University of Pennsylvania Law School, have only a 14 percent correlation with students' first-year grades. Moreover, these scores do not correlate at all with conventional success as measured in terms of income, self-reported satisfaction, and service contributions. In a recent study of its graduates over a thirty-year period, Harvard University found only two correlates of its successful graduates, where success was defined in terms of high income, community involvement, and a satisfying career. Those correlates were blue-color background and *low* SAT scores. Interestingly, SAT scores turn out to be more predictive of family income (80%), and would work very well, if the overriding goal of prestigious colleges and universities was simply to admit students from wealthy families.

So while prestigious colleges and universities maintain that they should be admitting the most qualified applicants into their schools, given their flawed evaluation procedure, they continue to accept a good number of applicants they should be rejecting and reject a good number of applicants they should be accepting.[11]

Compare this relatively poor success rate of standard admission procedures with what at our hypothetical elite university would be the relatively high success rate of remedial affirmative action program with respect to its goal of appropriately compensating those who have been discriminated against by proven past discrimination. Given the widespread racial discrimination in U.S. society, it would be relatively rare for a remedial affirmative action program to actually go awry and compensate persons who do not deserve to be so compensated. Unlike the weak correlation between SAT scores and being among the most qualified applicants (as evidenced by the 18% correlation with first year college grades), the correlation between being selected as a remedial affirmative action candidate and actually suffering from relevant past discrimination or the effects thereof must be extremely high.

It seems unconscionable, therefore, to fault remedial affirmative action programs for not having a foolproof way of ensuring that no one is compensated for past discrimination who is not the victim of the relevant past discrimination, given that the standard admissions procedures at elite colleges and universities that are only tenuously connected to their professed goals, and thus pass over many of their most qualified applicants for admission. As long as we tolerate a school admissions selection process at elite colleges and universities that are so faulty at picking out their most qualified applicants for admission, surely we should be more than tolerant of remedial affirmative action programs at those same colleges and universities that would succeed quite well at achieving their goal of compensating just those who have suffered from proven past discrimination or the effects thereof.

Fourth Objection

In support of the fourth objection that diversity affirmative action benefits the wrong people, James Fishkin claims that it benefits the most qualified, those who are actually the least deserving because they are the least discriminated against.[12] Yet the most qualified, who benefit from affirmative action in the United States, may not have been subjected to less discrimination; they may simply have resisted discrimination more vigorously. Even supposing that the most qualified were subject to less discrimination in the past, why wouldn't affirmative action be the appropriate response to the degree of discrimination to which they were subjected? If we assume that remedial affirmative action is only provided to those candidates whose qualifications are such that when their selection or appointment is actually combined with a suitably designed educational enhancement program, they will normally turn out, within a reasonably short time, to be as qualified as, or even more qualified than, their peers, then remedial affirmative action does seem to be appropriately directed at the most qualified candidates among those who have suffered from past discrimination. More severe forms of discrimination, whose effects upon a person's qualifications and potential are even more detrimental, may require correctives other than affirmative action, such as remedial education and job-training programs. Moreover, those forms of remedial affirmative action, which involve opening up entry-level positions to women and minorities, as in the construction industry, would benefit those who have suffered from the more severe forms of discrimination and so are even more deserving of compensation.

Nevertheless, if remedial affirmative action is to be justified in the United States, we will need to restrict the beneficiaries of remedial affirmative action that aims at compensating for past discrimination and its effects to those who continue to suffer from the effects of historic injustices, that is, to restrict it primarily to African Americans, American Indians, Hispanic Americans, and women. Other types of affirmative action that aim at outreach, putting an end to existing discrimination, and achieving diversity can be justifiably used more widely to benefit minorities and women generally as they are needed to achieve the ultimate goals of a colorblind, a gender-free, and an equal opportunity society.

Fifth Objection

Remedial affirmative action has also been criticized for being illegal in violation of the Civil Rights Act of 1964. According to the Act,

> No person in the United States shall, on the grounds of race, color, or national origin, be excluded from participation in, be denied the benefits of, or

be subjected to discrimination under any program or activity receiving Federal financial assistance.

The Civil Rights Act clearly prohibits racial preferences that exclude or discriminate, but it should not be taken to prohibit all forms of racial preferences because that would mean that it would prohibit just those very racial preferences that are needed to correct for violations of the Act itself, thus making its enforcement impossible.

Think of a law that prohibits the use of coercion in a certain context. Surely, that law should not be taken to prohibit whatever coercion is necessary to correct violations of the law itself. If it did that, then the law's prohibition of coercion would be unenforceable. Just as sometimes we need to use coercion to correct the violations of laws that prohibit the use of coercion, so sometimes we need to use racial preferences/classifications to enforce or correct for violations of laws, such as the Civil Rights Act, which prohibits the use of racial preferences/classifications. Furthermore, even racial proportionality can be used in a remedial affirmative action program, so as not to violate the Civil Rights Act of 1964, as we saw in the case of *Local 28 of the Sheet Metal Workers' International v. EEOC* (1986).

Accordingly, what the Civil Rights Act has to be taken as prohibiting is not all racial and sexual preferences, but only those racial and sexual preferences that are illegitimate. For example, it cannot be seen as ruling out a preference to have at least one qualified woman and one qualified minority on the U.S. Supreme Court.

Nevertheless, there is one Supreme Court decision that, as some critics of remedial affirmative action have claimed, may be interpreted as a violation of the Civil Rights Act of 1964. It is the Court's six-to-two decision in *United Steelworkers of America v. Weber* (1979). The facts of the case are as follows. Blacks represented 39 percent of the local population in Gramercy, Louisiana, but only 2 percent of the craft workers and 15 percent of the unskilled workers at the plant, up from 10 percent in 1969 when the company began to hire unskilled workers at the gate on a "one white, one black" basis. At the same time, the company continued its practice of hiring skilled craft workers from virtually all-white craft unions outside the Gramercy area, which accounted for the small percentage of minorities in craft positions at the plant. Under pressure from the federal government, Kaiser Aluminum and the unions agreed to jointly manage a craft apprenticeship program would accept one minority worker and one white worker from two different seniority lists until the percentage of minority workers approximated the percentage of minorities in the Gramercy area.

In this case, Justice Brennan, writing for the majority, distinguished between what the Civil Rights Act of 1964 forbids and what it permits. What the Act forbids, Brennan argued, is imposed racial preferences in certain context; what it permits are voluntary ones, like those found in the "voluntary" agreement between Kaiser Aluminum and the unions.

Now I admit that the Supreme Court's decision in this case does constitute a strained interpretation of the Civil Rights Act of 1964. This is because it is not clear that all voluntary racial preferences of this sort are legitimate. I would just want to point out that the Court's decision here was affected by the way the case had been brought before it. Neither Kaiser Aluminum, nor the unions, nor Weber who brought suit against the apprenticeship program, was interested in justifying the program as a means for putting an end to discrimination at the Gramercy plant. Consequently, the case was argued and decided on other grounds. But it could have been argued and decided on remedial grounds in the same way that a lower court in *Contractors Association of Eastern Pennsylvania v. the Secretary of Labor* (1973) had dealt with the Philadelphia Plan.

In that case, the federal court was concerned with a five-county Philadelphia area where minorities made up 30 percent of all construction workers but only 1 percent of the workers in six craft unions. The federal government's Philadelphia Plan conditioned the granting of federal construction money upon accepting a set of goals and timetables for improving minority apprenticeship or membership with respect to these unions. The federal court found the Philadelphia Plan to be an acceptable way of increasing equal opportunity for minorities in the Philadelphia area. Since in *Weber v. Kaiser Aluminum* (1979), the factual situation is quite similar, it could have been argued and decided on similar remedial grounds, and thus Justice Brennan's strained interpretation of the Civil Rights Act could have been avoided altogether.

Remedial affirmative action has also been criticized for being unconstitutional in violation of the Fourteenth Amendment and recent Supreme Court decisions. Part of the critique is similar to the one raised in the previous objection and can be responded to similarly. It assumes that defenders of remedial affirmative action are inappropriately defending group rights. Group rights, it is claimed, are not protected by the U.S. Constitution, particularly by the Equal Protection Clause of the Fourteenth Amendment, which applies to every single person individually and not as a member of a group. But, of course, the Equal Protection Clause does apply to individuals as members of the group of U.S. citizens, or U.S. residents. What the Equal Protection Clause does not do is apply to individuals simply as members of certain racial groups.[13] However we have already ruled out such membership as the appropriate moral grounds for remedial affirmative action, so there is no problem at all here ruling it out as appropriate constitutional grounds as well.

Attempting to further their critique on constitutional grounds, critics have pointed out that the Supreme Court in recent decisions has required that remedial affirmative action be based on proven discrimination specified by a judicial, legislative, or administrative finding.[14] But this raises no obstacle to defenders of remedial affirmative action. They should have no problem limiting it to proven discrimination, even though they would quibble a bit about who is capable of making an appropriate finding of discrimination. However, no one is interested in compensating for "societal discrimination" understood here as unproven discrimination.

7

A Defense of Diversity Affirmative Action

Unlike remedial affirmative action, diversity affirmative action is not grounded in the ideal of remedying discrimination, whether present or past. Rather its goal is diversity, which in turn is justified in terms of either the educational benefits it provides or its ability to create a more effective work force in such areas as policing and community relations, or achieving equal opportunity. The legal roots of this form of affirmative action in the United States are most prominent in *Regents of the University of California v. Bakke* (1978).

In *Bakke,* Justice Powell argued that the attainment of a diverse student body was clearly a constitutionally permissible goal for an institution of higher education. According to Powell, in an admissions program that aimed at diversity,

> [r]ace or ethnic background may be deemed a "plus" in a particular applicant's file, yet it does not insulate the individual from comparison with all other candidates for the available seats.... The applicant who loses out in

the last available seat to another candidate receiving a "plus" on the basis of ethnic background will not have been foreclosed from all consideration for that seat.... It will mean only that his combined qualifications... did not outweigh those of the other applicant.

Furthermore, an admissions program may "pay some attention to distribution among many types and categories of students," as more than a "token number of blacks" is needed to secure the educational benefits that flow from a racially and ethnically diverse student body.

For almost twenty years, Powell's opinion in *Bakke,* supported by Justices Brennan, Marshall, Blackman, and White, has been the rationale for the affirmative action used by most American colleges and universities. Even Justice O'Connor, who has rejected diversity as a compelling interest for the broadcasting industry in *Metro Broadcasting Inc. v. FCC* (1990), allowed in that decision that a state interest in the promotion of racial diversity has been found sufficiently compelling at least in the context of higher education.

In 1996, the U.S. Court of Appeals for the Fifth Circuit held in *Hopwood v. Texas* that Powell's opinion in *Bakke* is not a binding precedent. According to the Court, the view that race may be used as a "plus" factor to obtain diversity "garnered only [Powell's] vote and has never represented the view of a majority of the Court in *Bakke* or any other case." However, it has been generally recognized that the Brennan group (which included Brennan, who wrote the opinion, as well as Marshall, Blackmun, and White, who endorsed it) supported Powell's view. In fact, Brennan himself said as much in a subsequent decision. The reason no other case has supported Powell's view on diversity in education is that no other case since *Bakke* has dealt with diversity in education.

The *Hopwood* Court also ruled that evidence of discrimination in Texas's school system as a whole was not relevant to whether the affirmative action program of the University of Texas Law School is justified. Even though, as of May of 1994, desegregation suits remained pending against more than forty Texas school districts and, at the time the Hopwood plaintiffs filed suit, the U.S. Office of Civil Rights had not yet determined that the state had desegregated its schools sufficiently to comply with federal civil rights laws, and, even though most of the applicants to the Law School had passed through that very same educational system with its alleged inequalities, the *Hopwood* Court only allowed the Law School at the University of Texas to use evidence of its *own* discrimination to justify engaging in affirmative action.[1] But, as I have argued earlier, once sufficient evidence of discrimination has been provided, there seems to be no reason to impose the additional requirement that the agent engaged in the affirmative action program must be further implicated in the discrimination it is seeking to correct.

Interestingly, the Court based its overall decision on two contradictory claims about race.[2] First, the Court claimed that race does make a difference, that we can't assume there would be proportional participation in the absence of past discrimination. But the Court also claimed that race does not make a difference, that it is not a good indicator of diversity. Now we might try to rescue the Court from contradiction here by understanding its first claim about race to refer to an ideal society, and its second to refer to current U.S. society. So understood, the Court would be claiming that in an ideal society, race would still make a difference, but in our present society, race does not make a difference. But this would only save the Court from a contradiction by committing it to an absurdity. What we should believe about actual and ideal societies is exactly the opposite of what the Court appears to be claiming. What we should believe about the United States, based on the evidence of past and present discrimination, is that race does make a difference in the kind of life people experience in the United States. And what we should believe, or at least hope for, about an ideal society is that in such a society race will not make a difference because in such a society race will be no more significant than eye color is in most societies. Thus, the *Hopwood* Court's decision, based as it is on two contradictory conceptions of race, is deeply flawed.

The Michigan Cases

In Michigan in 2000 and 2001, there were two district court cases which reached diametrically opposed opinions about the legitimacy of using race as a factor to achieve diversity. In *Gratz v. Bollinger* (2000), the District Court for the Eastern District of Michigan held that under *Bakke,* diversity constitutes a compelling governmental interest that, in the context of education, justifies the use of race as one factor in the admissions process.

The Court ruled that the university had provided solid evidence regarding the educational benefits that flow from a racially and ethnically diverse student body.[3] Accordingly, the Court found that the university's undergraduate admissions program from 1999 to the present satisfies the *Bakke* requirements for a permissible race-conscious affirmative action program. That program uses a 150-point scale and assigns 20 points for membership in one of the identified underrepresented minority categories, as well as points for other factors such as athletics (20 points), and socioeconomic status (20 points), up to a total of 40 points for such factors.[4] At the same time, the Court found that an earlier program from 1995 to 1998, which protected a certain number of seats for athletes, foreign applicants, underrepresented minorities, ROTC candidates, and legacies, did fail the *Bakke* test, but only with respect to its *minority* set-aside. The other set-asides were legally permissible.

By contrast, another judge from the same District Court ruled in *Grutter v. Bollinger* (2001) that using race as a factor to achieve diversity was not established as a compelling state interest in *Bakke* because the Brennan group did not endorse the parts of Powell's opinion that discussed diversity. The Court quotes the Brennan group as saying that it "joins Part I and V-C of…Powell's opinion." Yet right after saying this, the Brennan group goes on to say, "We also agree with Justice Powell that a plan like the 'Harvard' plan is constitutional.…" Since the Harvard plan also sets out the diversity rationale for racial preference, it seems unreasonable to claim that the Brennan group is not endorsing this aspect of Powell's opinion.[5] As one would expect, however, having denied that Powell's support of racial diversity in education is a controlling precedent, the Court goes on to reject the affirmative action program at the Law School of the University of Michigan as unconstitutional.[6] However, this decision was reversed by the U.S. Court of Appeals for the Sixth Circuit in 2002, and both Michigan decisions were subsequently reviewed by the Supreme Court.

In 2003, the Supreme Court handed down its decisions on the Michigan cases. In both decisions a majority held that it is constitutionally permissible to use racial preferences to achieve the educational benefits of diversity. In *Grutter v. Bollinger,* the majority approved the University of Michigan Law School's way of achieving those benefits. In *Gratz v. Bollinger,* the majority rejected the university's way of achieving those benefits for its undergraduate program.

Without a doubt, the most important finding of the Court was the constitutional permissibility to use racial preferences to achieve the educational benefits of diversity. That, of course, had been the opinion of Justice Powell in *Bakke* (1978). But, as we have noted, there has been considerable debate about whether Powell's opinion represents the holding of the Court in *Bakke.* In *Grutter,* Justice Sandra Day O'Connor, writing for the majority, cut short that discussion by adopting the opinion of Powell in *Bakke* as the opinion of the majority in *Grutter:* "Today, we hold that the Law School has a compelling interest in attaining a diverse student body." By doing this, the Court also deferred to "the Law School's educational judgment that such diversity is essential to its educational mission." The grounds for this deference is the First Amendment's protection of educational autonomy, which secures the right of a university "to select those students who will contribute to the 'robust exchange of ideas' [quoting Powell]." At the same time, the Court is moved by evidence of the educational benefits of diversity provided by the Law School and by briefs of the *amici curiae* (friends of the court):

> American businesses have made clear that the skills needed in today's increasingly global marketplace can only be developed through exposure to widely diverse people, cultures, ideas, and viewpoints.
>
> What is more, high-ranking retired officers and civilian leaders of the United States military assert that "[biased on [their] decades of experience," a "highly qualified, racially diverse officer corps...is essential to the military's ability to fulfill its principle mission to provide national security."

Yet while affirming the constitutional permissibility of using racial preferences to achieve the educational benefits of diversity, the Supreme Court in *Grutter* accepted the Law School's affirmative action admissions program at the same time that the court in *Gratz* rejected the undergraduate school's program.

The difference between the two programs, according to the majority in *Grutter,* is that the undergraduate program, by automatically assigning twenty points on the basis of race or ethnicity, operated in a too-mechanical, nonindividualized manner. If race or ethnicity is to be a factor in admissions, the majority contends, there needs to be "individualized consideration of each and every applicant." The Law School, seeking to admit

350 students from 3,500 applicants, had used a more individualized admissions process that the court has now endorsed. The College of Literature, Science, and the Arts, facing the task of admitting 5,000 of 25,000 applicants, had chosen a more mechanical admissions process, still believing that it was sufficiently individualized to meet the Court's requirement of strict scrutiny. Now the Court ruled that its requirement of strict scrutiny, which demands that any use of race or ethnicity in admissions be narrowly tailored to achieve the educational benefits of diversity, cannot be met unless each applicant's qualifications are individually considered.

What the Law School in its individualized pursuit of the benefits of diversity had done is judge that racial diversity, at least for our times, is a very important means for achieving that goal, and further that racial diversity required a critical mass of minority students (where a critical mass is the number of students sufficient to enable under-represented minority students to contribute to class dialogue without feeling isolated—in my judgment this number is three to five for a class of thirty). Nor is critical mass a quota because it is fixed by the requirements of educational pedagogy, not to achieve a certain percentage of under-represented minority students in the entering class.

Predictably, the Supreme Court's decision in *Grutter* has met with two specific objections. Some deny that the educational benefits of diversity are an important enough state purpose to justify the use of racial preferences to achieve them. Others allow that the educational benefits of diversity are an important enough state purpose to justify the use of racial preferences: they just contend that there are other means that are preferable because they can achieve the same educational benefits of diversity in a race-neutral way. In the following section, I examine and respond to each of these objections.

Diversity Not Important Enough

In its brief before the Supreme Court in the Michigan cases, the Michigan Association of Scholars maintained that "even where diversity in their classrooms is a genuine merit, it is simply not the case that their work, their teaching, their research, cannot go forward successfully in its absence."[7] When making this claim, however, opponents of affirmative action must not be thinking about what happens in classrooms when racial issues are discussed, or analogously, what happens in classrooms when gender issues are discussed.[8] Surely, the teachers among us who have led discussions on racial issues in our classrooms, both with and without minority students being present, know what a significant difference the presence of minorities makes in such contexts. Similarly there is a loss when gender issues are discussed in the absence of women. Thus, when opponents of affirmative action maintain that diversity is unnecessary for successful teaching, they must not be thinking about courses focused on racial (or gender) issues, but rather about courses where the subject matter is logic, math, or physics, or something similar. But even in such courses, diversity can have a significant impact.

I am reminded of the jarring impact my partner—a fast-talking, chain-smoking New Yorker—had on her logic students who were Mormon, particularly the men in her class, as the first woman in the philosophy department at the University of Utah in the early 1970s. Years later I noted the impact that the only minority student in my class of thirty had on her classmates when I asked her to read her well-written paper in which she described visiting her wealthy white relatives on Thanksgiving only to have a rock thrown through their dining room window while they were there. Accordingly, it is difficult to deny the significant educational benefits that minorities and women bring to colleges and universities, especially, but not exclusively, when racial and gender issues are being discussed.

Nevertheless, without denying the educational benefits of diversity, it still might be argued that achieving those benefits does not constitute an important enough state purpose to justify the use of racial preferences to secure them. This would seem to be the position of Justice Thomas in his dissent in the *Grutter* case. Thomas argues that the only kind of state purpose that would be important enough to justify the use of racial preferences in a nonremedial context is national security or, more broadly, "measures the State must take to provide a bulwark against anarchy, or to prevent violence." In the *Grutter* case, no one, except Justice Scalia, joined Thomas in defending such an extreme limitation on the use of racial preferences.

Both Thomas and Scalia also argue that the Michigan Law School could secure the educational benefits of diversity without using racial preferences by simply giving up on its goal of being an elite law school. To further show that the Michigan Law School was not serving any compelling state purpose, Thomas noted that although the school accounts for nearly

30 percent of all law students graduating in Michigan, only 6 percent of its graduates take the bar exam in the state, and only 16 percent elect to stay in the state. By contrast, Wayne State University Law School is said to send "88% of its graduates on to serve the people of Michigan."

But, of course, percentages don't tell the whole story here, and Thomas neglected to assess how well-placed and influential those 6 percent or 16 percent turn out to be. Moreover, the suggestion that Michigan could not have a compelling state interest in doing something that primarily benefits the rest of the country is extremely odd. It is like saying that Michigan could not have a compelling state interest in controlling the sulfur admissions of its power plants that causes, let's suppose, much of the acid rain that negatively affects New England states.

Still, a central issue remains whether Michigan should have to choose between having an elite law school and having the educational benefits of diversity. Thomas and Scalia argue that Michigan must make this choice because to do otherwise would involve using racial preferences in a way that is prohibited by the Equal Protection Clause of the Fourteenth Amendment. By contrast, the majority in *Grutter* contends that Michigan is not forced to make this choice—that it can have a law school that is both elite and diverse—because the use of racial preferences to achieve the educational benefits of diversity is permitted by the Equal Protection Clause.

The key question here is: Whose interpretation of the Equal Protection Clause of the Fourteenth Amendment should we accept? The majority, to support their interpretation of the Amendment, could have appealed to the original intent of the Congress that formulated and passed it.[9] As I noted before, the same Congress that formulated and passed the Fourteenth Amendment also formulated and passes race-conscious statutes that provided schools and farmland to both free blacks and former slaves. In fact, this same Congress viewed its passing of the Fourteenth Amendment as a necessary means of supporting the legality of its race-conscious statutes. However, rather than appeal to the original intent of the Amendment, the majority in *Grutter* relies on an interpretation by a number of Supreme Court cases in the last fifty years or so.[10]

The history of this interpretation is usually traced to *Korematsu v. United States* (1944), with Justice Harlon Stone's note in *United States v. Carolene Products Co.* (1938) sometimes cited as an earlier source. In *Korematsu,* Justice Hugo Black while upholding the constitutionality of the interment of the Japanese Americans during World War II on grounds of national security held that "all legal restrictions which curtail the civil rights of a single racial group are immediately suspect. That is not to say that all such restrictions are unconstitutional. It is to say that courts must subject them to the most rigid scrutiny."[11] Using this interpretation of the Equal Protection Clause of the Fourteenth Amendment, the Supreme Court in a number of decisions prior to *Brown v. Board of Education of Topeka, Kansas* (1954), struck down state laws segregating blacks and whites but only because the segregated facilities were not of equal quality.

In *Brown* the Supreme Court went further, ruling that the legally required separation of the races cannot be equal, and demanding the desegregation of public schools on the grounds that the separation of blacks and whites is motivated by and reinforces attitudes of racial superiority. In so acting, the Court emphasized the invidious nature of this use of racial preferences. In *Regents of the University of California v. Bakke* (1978), however, the Court faced a use of racial preferences that appeared to be motivated, not by invidious intent, but rather by a desire to remedy past wrongs. In a fractured decision, a majority of Powell and the Brennan group held that race can be used as a factor in admission decisions. But another majority of Powell and the Stevens group held that the appropriate standard for evaluating the use of racial preferences is strict scrutiny. According to this standard, there must be a compelling state interest (which in this case Powell took to be diversity), and the use of racial preferences in pursuit of that interest must be narrowly tailored.

It is Powell's approach in *Bakke* that has come to be endorsed in a number of subsequent Supreme Court decisions, including the *Grutter* decision. Thus, in *Grutter,* O'Connor writes:

> We have held that all racial classifications imposed by government must be analyzed by the reviewing court under strict scrutiny.

O'Connor also adds, quoting herself in *Adarand Constuctors, Inc. vs. Pena* (1995), that strict scrutiny need not be "fatal in fact." This is just where the disagreement between the majority in *Grutter* and Thomas and Scalia is joined. In *Adarand,* Thomas had claimed with Scalia in agreement:

> Government-sponsored racial discrimination based on benign prejudice is just as noxious as discrimination inspired by malicious prejudice.

In *Grutter,* Thomas reiterates basically the same claim, making it clear that his grounds for rejecting all racial preferences are the bad consequences that result from their use. In Thomas's view, the state of Michigan would be better off with a law school that is diverse but not elite than it is with its existing law school, which is both diverse and elite. Unfortunately, neither Thomas nor Scalia bother to set out the required consequentialist argument to show that this is the case.[12] And it is surely the failure of Thomas or Scalia to provide the necessary consequentialist argument, along with Michigan's Gurin Report and over 100 amici curiae briefs attesting to the benefits of affirmative action, that persuaded O'Connor to join with the more liberal side of the Court in this case.[13]

But what if there was a way to oppose the use of racial preferences in the affirmative action program at the University of Michigan that doesn't require us to weigh the consequences of using racial preferences? Terence Pell believes that he has found such a way.[14] Pell claims that the University of Michigan's way of securing the educational benefits of diversity are opposed to an ideal of formal equality, which he claims is embedded in the Equal Protection Clause of the Fourteenth Amendment. According to Pell, this ideal of formal equality is procedural, like the due process requirements in the criminal justice system. To reflect this ideal of formal equality, college and university admission systems must have the character of a fair procedure and not be governed by end-state-driven requirements such as diversity.

The problem with Pell's argument is that although there are some purely procedural requirements that should govern college and university admission systems—for example, the requirement that application forms be turned in by certain deadlines—most of the standards for admission, even the ones that Pell favors, are really end-state or end-state-driven requirements, not purely procedural ones. Take, for example, the GPA and standardized test scores requirements used by the University of Michigan. These standards are used in the hope of getting students who have sufficient academic ability to benefit from the University of Michigan's educational program. They are used as a means to achieve a certain end-state: a student body whose members have sufficient academic ability to benefit from the university's educational program.

When athletic preferences are introduced into the standards for admission, the goal that propels their use is to have high-quality sports teams at educational institutions. When geographical preferences are introduced, the goal is to have a significant degree of geographical representation (usually home state representation for state schools). And, of course, when racial preferences are introduced, the goal is to achieve the educational benefits of diversity. Thus, all of these standards governing admission are end-state or end-state driven standards.[15] What this shows is that there is no way to contrast a standard for admission that uses racial preferences with other standards for admission on the grounds that the racial standard aims to achieve an end-state but the others do not. All the standards used in admission decisions except for a few, like the purely procedural application deadline requirements, are end-state or end-state driven standards; they all aim to achieve certain desirable end-states.

So if we cannot use Pell's procedural/end-state distinction to provide a formal way of showing that the use of racial preferences to achieve the educational benefits of diversity violates the Equal Protection Clause of the Fourteenth Amendment, we are really driven back to the consequentialist evaluation required by Powell's strict scrutiny standard in *Bakke* and in subsequent decisions. We are then required to assess the impact of using specific racial preferences in various contexts, ultimately trying to determine whether their overall consequences are not only good and important, but better than the available alternatives, while at the same time ensuring that the use of racial preferences does not impose an invidious burden on anyone.

Again, what is crucially at issue here is when racial preferences are legitimate and when they are illegitimate. No one in their right mind thinks that racial preferences are always legitimate or always illegitimate.

There Are Better Means

It is easy to see that the claim that there are better means, typically race-neutral ones, is just another way of continuing the consequentialist evaluation required by the strict scrutiny standard.[16] The Texas 10 Percent Plan and the Florida 20 Percent Plan are usually put forward by opponents of affirmative action as race-neutral ways of securing the educational benefits of diversity. Likewise, class-based programs of affirmative action have been defended as preferable to race-based ones. Let us consider both alternatives.

The Texas 10 Percent Plan and the Florida 20 Percent Plan are now successfully admitting minorities into their undergraduate institutions at levels that either match, or, in Florida's case, surpass what they had accomplished with race-based affirmative action programs. This was not accomplished, however, without a substantial increase in scholarship aid for minorities, and without, in the case of Texas, using smaller classes and a variety of remedial programs.[17] Both plans also rely on at least de facto segregated high schools in their respective states to produce the diversity they have. If the high schools in both states were in fact more integrated, the plans would not be as effective as they are with respect to undergraduate enrollment.

Even so the plans employed still had serious drawbacks. First, they did nothing for law and medical schools, and for other graduate and professional schools ending affirmative action has been devastating. African American enrollment at the University of Texas Law School dropped from 5.8 percent (twenty-nine students) in 1996 to 0.9 percent (six students) in 1997. It rose to 1.8 percent (nine students) in 1998 and then fell to 1.7 percent (nine students) in 1999. Since then, there has been improvement in the number of African Americans enrolled at the University of Texas Law School, although the numbers have yet to approach pre-*Hopwood* levels. This holds true for most other University of Texas professional schools as well.

Second, the Texas Plan has a detrimental effect on the admission of minorities not in the top 10 percent, who might have been admitted pre-*Hopwood*. Minority students who are not in the top 10 percent of their high school graduating classes have little hope of admission under the Texas Plan. Third, such plans restrict universities from doing the individualized assessments that would be required to assemble a student body that is not only racially diverse, but also diverse in other ways. Fourth, an analysis of data from the Florida Plan showed that students at seventy-five of Florida's high schools could have carried a C+ average and still have ranked in the top 20 percent of their class. Fifth, such plans only work, if at all, for universities that admit primarily from a statewide population. Only 11 percent of the applicants to the University of Texas at Austin are nonresidents whereas many elite colleges and universities recruit students from a national and international pool, and thus cannot apply the percent model to their selection of student bodies.

There is yet another reason that may trump all the others as a reason for rejecting these so-called alternatives to a race-based affirmative action. It is that despite their claims to be race-neutral, these percentage-plan alternatives are really race-based themselves. They are means that are chosen explicitly because they are thought to produce a desirable degree of racial diversity. In this regard, they are no different from the poll-taxes that were used in the segregated South, which were purportedly race-neutral means, but were clearly designed to produce an objectionable racial result—to keep blacks from voting.[18] Accordingly, if we are going to end up using a race-based selection procedure to get the educational benefits of diversity, we might as well use one that most effectively produces that desired result, and that is a selection procedure that explicitly employs race as a factor in admissions.

It is not surprising, therefore, that is exactly what the University of Texas proposed to do once the Supreme Court's *Grutter* decision nullified the *Hopwood*'s authority. The university has also sought to limit the 10 Percent Plan to 50–60 percent of its incoming class, down from the more than 70 percent that have been admitted under the plan. Although this attempt to limit the 10 Percent Plan was rebuffed by the state legislature in 2007, the university is now using racial preference to the degree that is consistent with abiding by the Plan.[19]

What this shows is that the practitioners of the most highly regarded alternative to affirmative action in the country, those very same people who were in the best position to assess its merits and limitations, now want to use affirmative action and in other ways restrict and go beyond the 10 Percent Plan. That seems to me to be very strong evidence against the viability of the Texas Plan and the Florida Plan as alternatives to affirmative action.

Unimpressed with percentage plans, Richard Kalenberg has proposed that affirmative action programs should be based on class rather than race. Kalenberg contends that class-based affirmative action is an appropriate substitute for race- and sex-based affirmative action; he wants the benefits that affirmative action provides to go to those who are disadvantaged by the socioeconomic class to which they belong.[20] In his attempt to provide an alternative to race-based affirmative action, Kalenberg favors a complex measure of social and economic disadvantage, similar to the one that UCLA Law School has employed in response to Proposition 209.

The UCLA Law School looked at three family factors (an applicant's family income, father's education, and mother's education) and three neighborhood factors (proportion of single-parent households, proportion

of families receiving welfare, and proportion of adults who had not graduated from high school). Using this measure of social and economic disadvantage in its class-based affirmative action program, the UCLA Law
School was more successful than Berkeley's Boalt Hall Law School in
maintaining racial diversity in its entering class. Still, because of Proposition 209, black enrollment at UCLA Law School dropped 72 percent in
comparison to pre-*Hopwood* averages.

However, Kalenberg favors adding even more factors than the UCLA
Law School used to measure social and economic disadvantage. For example, he suggests including net family wealth and accepting even lower SAT
scores. But even such measures would not be enough to capture the disadvantage that minorities—particularly African Americans—experience,
such as the unjustified lower expectations of some of their teachers and
the stereotype threat when taking standardized cognitive tests.[21] In prin-
ciple, it should be possible to break down racial disadvantage into a set
of factors that does not include the fact that a person is a member of a
particular racial group.[22] Nevertheless, if the measure of racial disadvantage is to be adequate, it may well have to include such facts as "being
discriminated against simply for being a member of a particular minority
group," just as any adequate measure of women's disadvantage that is due
to sexism may have to include such facts as "being discriminated against
simply because one is a woman."[23]

Moreover, even if it turned out that African Americans and whites
with, say, the same net wealth have the same grade point averages and
SAT scores, for any particular level of net wealth (even low levels), there
are presently disproportionately more whites at that level than there are
African Americans, Given that the number of admission slots available for
diversity affirmative action is usually limited, neutrally selecting those to
be admitted based on net family wealth other things being equal, would
necessarily result in considerably fewer African Americans thereby being
admitted. For this reason, class-based affirmative action cannot serve as a
suitable proxy for race-based affirmative action.[24]

Diversity Affirmative Action to Achieve Equal Opportunity

Nevertheless, there are good reasons to expand diversity affirmative
action—especially in higher education—to extend to the economically

disadvantaged, not as a substitute for race-based affirmative action, but rather as an addition to it with the aim of securing more equal opportunity in society.

Consider the following:

- Although the median U.S. family income today is a little over $54,000 per year, but almost 90 percent of Harvard students come from families with greater incomes, and almost 75 percent of Harvard students come from families with incomes over $100,000.[25]
- Although fewer than 2 percent of U.S. families have incomes more than $250,000, 20 percent of first-year students at Northwestern University come from such families.[26]
- Of the students attending Notre Dame, Northwestern, Penn, Harvard, Princeton, Virginia, and Washington University in St. Louis less than 10 percent come from families earning less than $40,000 a year so as to qualify for Pell grants.[27]
- At top elite colleges, only 3 percent come from the bottom quarter of U.S. family incomes.[28]

So, for the most part, elite U.S. colleges that are supported with federal dollars and tax-exempt status are primarily attended by children from the wealthiest families.

Also consider the following:

- Most nonacademic admission preferences disproportionately benefit white, wealthy applicants.[29]
- Although it is generally believed that athletic preferences disproportionately favor minority students, this is not the case. More than counterbalancing minority participation in basketball, football, and track is participation mainly by upper-income whites in such sports as horseback riding, skiing, sailing, fencing, golf, crew, squash, and even polo at Cornell and Virginia.[30]
- According to one study, legacy applicants received an average of 47 extra points on their SATs, according to another—160. Underrepresented minorities and athletes receive an average of 108 extra points.[31]
- Half of Notre Dame's legacy admits each year would not have been admitted without the preference they received for being legacies.[32]
- At Ivy League and other elite schools, legacies make up as much as 25 percent of the student body.[33]
- Students without any nonacademic preference are vying for only 40 percent of the slots at the elite schools.[34]

So the major beneficiaries of preferences at elite colleges in the United States turn out to be white students from wealthy or relatively wealthy families.

Putting these two "considerations" together, elite colleges in the United States are supported with federal dollars and tax-exempt status, while the students attending those colleges, almost exclusively, come from wealthy or relatively wealthy families, and a good number of them are admitted either as legacies or because they play esoteric sports that only students from wealthy or relatively wealthy families would normally have the opportunity to learn to play.

It is not surprising, therefore, that 75 percent of Americans oppose giving legacies "extra consideration for admission," according to the *Chronicle of Higher Education*.[35] In effect, elite colleges in the United States are functioning like country clubs for students from wealthy or the relatively wealthy families. Of course, there is nothing wrong in itself with the existence of institutions that are, or function like, country clubs for the rich. What is wrong, however, is when such institutions are supported with federal dollars and tax-exempt status. The needed corrective is a significant cut in legacy preferences at elite colleges, and replacing them with a corresponding number of preferences enabling more economically disadvantaged students to attend the same schools.

In the process of filling the slots at elite colleges opened up for economically disadvantaged students, it will be necessary to accept students with somewhat lower SAT scores and GPAs than would otherwise have been the required. Given the unequal K through 12 educational system in the United States, students who come from economically disadvantaged families cannot normally be expected to secure exactly the same academic credentials as those who are admitted to these schools without any preferential treatment. They should, however, tend to match the academic credentials of those students who previously had been admitted based on legacy or athletic preferences. Under such a program, only those students would be admitted whose qualifications are such that when their selection is combined with a suitably designed educational enhancement program, they will normally turn out, within a reasonably short time, to be as qualified as, or even more qualified than, their peers.

Of course, it will be objected that elite colleges need to employ legacy and other preferences for the rich in order to maintain their endowments.

As it turns out, legacy and other preferences for the rich are actually of fairly recent origin. Before World War I, although there was a tradition of alumni giving at elite colleges and universities, the children of alumni of elite colleges and universities did not need preferences.[36] Even Harvard and Yale were able to accept all those who passed their entrance exams and paid their tuitions. After the war, however, for a variety of reasons, the number of applications radically increased and legacy preferences were introduced at first to help suppress Jewish enrollment.[37]

Yet even today, there are elite schools that manage to maintain their endowments without legacy and other preferences for the rich. Cal Tech, possibly the best or second best engineering school in the United States, has done it, as have Oxford and Cambridge universities. Former vice president Al Gore's son, Albert, and former senate majority leader, Bill Frist's son Harrison, were each admitted as a legacy to their fathers' alma maters, Harvard and Princeton respectively, even though their academic credentials were considerably below the normal admission standards of those institutions. By contrast, former Prime Minister Tony Blair's son, Euan, was denied admission to Oxford, his father's alma mater, despite Euan's much better academic credentials.

In order to make the changes that are needed here people's expectations with respect to elite colleges and universities have to change. On the one hand, if rich people expect elite colleges and universities to give preference to their children simply because they are alumni/a, then, of course, they will be disappointed if their children are not accepted by those institutions. On the other hand, if rich people expect that elite colleges and universities will maintain their educational standards and goals irrespective of alumni/a connections, then, even if their children do not gain admission, they can still respect their alma maters for not turning themselves in country clubs for the rich, and for being more open to all applicants who can meet their academic standards and goals, and they can still remain grateful to them for the education they themselves received. Such changes in expectations and attitudes should be able to provide an alternative basis for maintaining and growing the endowments of elite colleges and universities.

In any case, policies at elite colleges and universities cannot continue primarily favoring the wealthy and relatively wealthy with legacy and other preferences while practically excluding almost everyone else. They cannot be run as country clubs for the rich while receiving from the government large outlays of federal dollars and tax-exempt status. To justifiably retain federal support and tax-exempt status, elite colleges and universities must transform themselves so that they are genuinely open to all qualified students. This will require putting an end to the favoritism shown to the rich and the relatively rich by instituting affirmative action programs for the economically disadvantaged that are at least as large as the race-based affirmative action programs that exist at those universities. The admissions slots needed for these new preferences for the economically disadvantaged are to be secured by a comparable cut in legacy preferences and other special preferences for the rich. As universities are able to successfully change the way they maintain and grow their endowments, it will then be possible to eliminate all legacy and other special preferences for the rich.

For some time now, there has been a vigorous debate going on in the United States over the justification of race- and sex-based affirmative action. While this debate has been raging in the halls of government, academia and beyond, there has been the equivalent of two 500-pound gorillas sitting right in the midst of the debaters that few of the participants seems to have noticed, especially the opponents of affirmative action. The two "gorillas" are legacy and athletic preferences for white, wealthy students. Taking these preferences for the rich into account and doing an appropriate assessment of them leads, I have argued, to the conclusion that they should be eliminated or reduced in favor of preferences for the economically disadvantaged, the latter being a form of diversity affirmative action that seeks to secure greater equal opportunity in society.

To sum up, diversity affirmative action should be regarded as justified when

1) Race is used as a factor to select from the pool of applicants a sufficient number of qualified applicants to secure the educational benefits that flow from a racially and ethnically diverse student body.
2) Preference is given to economically disadvantaged applicants by cutting legacy and other preferences for the rich and relatively rich at elite colleges and universities.
3) Only candidates are selected whose qualifications are such that when their selection is combined with a suitably designed educational enhancement program, they will normally turn out, within a reasonably short time, to be as qualified as, or even more qualified than, their peers.

8

OBJECTIONS TO DIVERSITY
AFFIRMATIVE ACTION

The diversity affirmative action that I have defended in chapter 7 has been criticized in various ways. Specifically, critics have claimed that this form of affirmative action is objectionable for the following reasons:

1) It harms those who receive it.
2) It is unfair to the white males against whom it discriminates.
3) It is illegal and unconstitutional.

Let me address each of these objections.

First Objection

In support of the first objection, Charles Murray claims that affirmative action harms those who receive it by placing women and minorities into positions for which they are not qualified.[1] Murray cites examples, from his personal experience and the personal experience of others, of women and minorities that were harmed in this way. In one example, a black woman is hired for a position for which she lacks the qualifications and, as a result, her responsibilities are reduced, making her job a dead-end position. Yet I have argued that when diversity affirmative action has such an effect, it is not justified. To be justified, diversity affirmative action must be directed at candidates whose qualifications are such that when their selection or appointment is combined with a suitably designed educational enhancement program, they will normally turn out, within a reasonably short time, to be as qualified as, or even more qualified than, their peers. So if diversity affirmative action is properly applied and carried out, it will not harm those who receive it.[2]

Nevertheless, there is another way that diversity affirmative action might be harmful to minorities. Thomas Sowell claims that affirmative action mismatches minorities with the colleges and professional schools they attend, such that a greater number of them perform unsatisfactorily than would otherwise be the case without affirmative action. To make this point, Sowell quotes at length from an article by Clyde Summers of Yale Law School:

> If Harvard or Yale, for example, admits minority students with test scores 100 to 150 points below that normally required for a nonminority student to get admitted, the total number of minority students able to get a legal education is not increased thereby. The minority students given such preference would meet the normal admissions standard at Illinois, Rutgers or Texas. Similarly, minority students given preference at Pennsylvania would meet normal standards at Pittsburgh, those given preference at Duke would meet normal standards at North Carolina, and those given preference at Vanderbilt would meet normal standards at Kentucky, Mississippi and West Virginia. Thus, each law school, by its preference admission, simply takes minority students away from other schools whose admissions standard are further down the scale.... In sum, the policy of preferential admission has a pervasive shifting effect, causing large numbers of minority students to attend law schools whose normal admissions standard they do not meet, instead of attending other law schools whose normal standards they do meet.[3]

Bowen and Bok attempt to meet this mismatching-leading-to-greater-failure argument by pointing out that the schools in their study have high graduation rates for minorities.[4] Sowell counters by claiming that Bowen and Bok's sample of twenty-four private and four public elite schools is atypical and that there are other elite schools, particularly elite public universities where the SAT gap between white and minority students is generally greater, leading to lower graduation rates for the latter.[5] But although there may be some elite schools where the SAT gap is greater, the gap does tend to be fairly constant over elite schools. In addition, if we look at the University of Michigan, an elite public school, we find that although there is a graduation gap for minorities, it is still a few percentage points higher than it is for whites graduating from all 305 large universities that participate in Division I-level NCAA athletics.[6] This would seem to suggest that the causes of the lower graduation rate among underrepresented minorities have little to do with whether those minorities benefited from diversity affirmative action.

There is, however, a recent study by Richard Sander that attempts to support Sowell's view that minorities are being harmed by affirmative action, at least at U.S. law schools.[7] Sander provides a statistical argument that affirmative action mismatches black students at law schools by admitting them with lower LSAT scores and undergraduate grades that put them at an academic disadvantage, thereby resulting in their having lower grades and lower rates of graduating and passing the bar. Sander further argues that if affirmative action ended, blacks would cascade to lower ranked schools where they would perform dramatically better, causing a net increase of 8 percent in the number of new black lawyers, and a 22 percent net increase in the number of blacks passing the bar on the first attempt.[8]

I myself critiqued Sander's argument in the same issue of the *Stanford Law Review* in which his article appeared in 2004. However, Sander's article went on to create so much controversy that the next year the *Review* published a special issue containing four critiques of it and a reply by Sander himself.

In his article, Sander argued that without affirmative action blacks would cascade to lower ranked law schools where they would get higher grades and have higher rates of graduation and bar passage. To determine how well cascading blacks would do at the lower-ranked schools, Sander assumed that blacks would do as well as whites with the similar LSAT scores and undergraduate grades, given that, according to Sander, LSAT

scores and undergraduate grades are the only relevant criteria for predict-
ing law school success. It is on this basis that Sander was able to claim that
blacks who receive affirmative action to attend a higher ranked law school
are "mismatched"—they would be better off if they had attended lower
ranked schools.

However, when some of Sander's critics proposed determining how
cascading blacks would do at the lower-ranked schools by more plausibly
assuming that they would do as well as blacks at those same schools were
doing with similar LSAT scores and undergraduate grades, Sander's statistical argument began to collapse. Under this assessment, it turned out
that cascading would not help blacks at all; they would do better if they,
in fact, remained at higher ranked schools as beneficiaries of affirmative
action.[9]

In his "Reply to Critics," Sander, attempting to salvage his argument,
granted that he should have been comparing blacks to blacks to determine
the benefits from cascading, but then claimed that blacks who he had
wrongly expected to be better off from cascading must have had "unobservable characteristics" that enabled them—even while experiencing the
"disadvantages" of affirmative action—to outperform blacks who were
at lower ranked schools where the cascading blacks seemed to belong.[10]
Yet while there are surely other factors involved in law school admission
other than just LSAT scores and undergraduate grades (the only factors
that Sander had initially recognized), Sander's treatment of such factors as
"unobservable characteristics" and his appealing to them when, and only
when, their absence would cast doubt on his argument against affirmative
action is surely too ad hoc an appeal to such factors to provide a defense of
his view.

Sander also recognizes that without affirmative action at elite law schools,
black enrollment would decline from around 8 percent to 1–2 percent.[11]
This is particularly significant given that 40 percent of the black lawyers
at top law firms and 48 percent of black law professors come from the top
ten law schools.[12] On his website, Sander also estimates that without affirmative action, there would be zero, or nearly zero, blacks at Harvard Law
School and Yale Law School. Again, this is particularly significant given
that 25 percent of black law professors in the United States have graduated
from those two law schools.[13] Thus, cascading would not help blacks presently attending elite law schools from which, Sander grants, 95.3 percent

graduate.[14] For Sander, the benefits from blacks cascading only occur for those blacks attending non-elite schools. Yet exactly how these benefits would overcome the losses that would occur from such a drastic decline in blacks enrolled at elite law schools, Sander never makes clear.

In any case, Sander maintains in his "Reply" that the impact eliminating affirmative action would have on the production of black lawyers (the 8 percent increase, he mentioned in his original article) is "really a side issue" and so no longer a central claim of his view.[15] Now his central thesis is simply that the rate of first time (but not eventual) bar passage will be higher for black law graduates with cascading. Yet why should we be concerned with such a meager payoff? Isn't what really counts in this regard is not the rate of first time bar passage but rather the rate of eventual bar passage? With respect to that outcome, Sander's critics argue (and Sander himself implicitly concedes by focusing on the rate of first-time passage) that ending affirmative action would have no impact at all.[16]

The real impact of ending affirmative action, Sander's critics contend, would be on the production of black lawyers.[17] According to one estimate there would be about a 21 percent drop.[18] This, of course, contrasts with Sander's initial claim, now abandoned in the "Reply," that ending affirmative action would produce an 8 percent increase of (non-elite) black lawyers. Nor does Sanders directly critique the 21 percent drop claim made by some of his critics. Rather, he allows that these critics are "strongest when discussing the consequences of eliminating racial preferences on the production of black lawyers."[19] So again, we need to ask exactly how blacks or black lawyers could be better off with a 21 percent drop in the production of black lawyers, and with a more than 75 percent drop in black lawyers graduating from elite law schools, especially in view of the positions that black graduates from just those elite schools have been acquiring on law school faculties and at top law firms. Sander never explains how this could be the case.

Second Objection

In support of the second objection, Barry Gross claims that affirmative action is unfair to nonminority males because it deprives them of equal opportunity by selecting or appointing women or minority candidates over more qualified nonminority male candidates.[20] Of course, we could reject the grounds for Gross's argument and maintain that the diversity that affirmative action candidates bring with them renders them as qualified, or even more qualified, than nonminority male candidates.

But for the sake of argument, let's grant that the affirmative action candidates are less qualified. Consider then the following two programs. Program A first hires women and minority candidates who are qualified but not as qualified or more qualified than nonminority male candidates and then puts them through a six-month training program, after which it lets go any trainees who are not as qualified as anyone else in the hiring pool. In contrast, Program B first admits highly qualified women and minority candidates into a six-month training program for which nonminority male candidates are not eligible, and then hires just those women and minority candidates who, after completing the program, are either as qualified, or more qualified, than anyone else in the hiring pool. Presumably, Gross would only object to Program A because only that program involves hiring women and minority candidates who are less qualified. But given that both Program A and Program B end up retaining exactly the same candidates, how could one program be objectionable but not the other? In fact, Gross should find both programs acceptable.[21] Recall too, that the diversity affirmative action that I defend only selects candidates whose qualifications are such that when their selection is combined with a suitably designed educational enhancement program, they will normally turn out, within a reasonably short time, to be as qualified as, or even more qualified than, their peers. So, Gross should have no reason to object to this form of diversity affirmative action.

Nevertheless, those who lost out to affirmative action candidates might see themselves as wronged by this policy. But how justified is this reaction? Surely, it would have no moral force against outreach affirmative action or against affirmative action that simply seeks to put an end to existing discrimination because while both these types of affirmative action may use race- and sex-based preferences, they only use them to create, possibly for the first time, an equal playing field. Surely, those who see themselves wronged by affirmative action should not be objecting to an equal playing field! It is also difficult to see how any white person could justifiably complain against an affirmative action program that aims to compensate for racial discrimination or its effects when, given the widespread racial discrimination that exists today (see chapter 1) almost any white person living today has most surely unjustly benefited from that discrimination. Thus, it would seem that the strongest case for those who claim to be wronged by affirmative action would have to be against diversity affirmative action. They would have to argue the benefits of diversity do not sufficiently outweigh the losses imposed on non–affirmative action candidates.[22] To better evaluate this argument, let us consider other preference programs and practices that are commonly regarded as justified in the United States.

Most relevant to diversity affirmative action in higher education are legacy and athletic preferences. In the United States, legacies constitute about 25 percent of the student body at select colleges and universities, and athletes constitute less than 5 percent of the male student body at a large school like Michigan but as much as 32 percent of smaller liberal arts colleges. A recent study by the U.S. Office of Civil Rights found that legacies admitted into Harvard were significantly less qualified than the average admitted nonlegacies. Yet rarely do people object to either of these forms of preference.[23] By contrast, those admitted based on racial preferences make up between 5 and 10 percent of the student body at select colleges and universities, and the objectors to this form of preference are legion.

Most relevant to diversity affirmative action in employment are veterans' preferences and nepotism. As part of veterans' preference in the United States, the federal government and most states add ten points to the civil service exam scores of disabled veterans or their wives, and five points to the scores of nondisabled veterans. After bonus points are added, veterans are often preferred over nonveterans with equal scores. Seven states give absolute preference to all veterans who pass their civil service exams. Veterans' preference in the United States is also lifelong. Even the Civil Rights Act of 1964 contains the following clause protecting veterans' preference: "Nothing contained…shall be construed to repeal or modify…special rights or preferences for veterans." It is also noteworthy that the generous veterans' preference enacted after World War II gave the same benefits to those who were drafted as to those who joined, to those who served overseas and saw combat as to those who never left the United States.[24] And while it might be claimed that veterans' preference is to some degree earned, nepotism, or preferring one's relatives in employment, is not, yet it is widely practiced in the United States, especially in small businesses. In any case, rarely does anyone object to veterans' preference or nepotism.

So if we regard these preferences as justified, why should we not similarly regard using racial preferences to achieve important educational benefits or a more effective work force as justified? It is also interesting how after the September 11, 2001 terrorist attacks on the World Trade Center and the Pentagon, the U.S. government has moved to use racial profiling (classifications) in a way that would not withstand strict scrutiny. But to use racial classifications with far more justification to achieve a colorblind (racially just) society is treated as something quite different.

Yet suppose you were against *all* of these forms of preference. In that case, you would need to rank them according to how objectionable each of them happens to be. In doing that, you would have to rank athletic and legacy preferences as the most objectionable. Failing to oppose them more strongly than racial preference (as most of those who claim to be against all forms of preferences tend to do) would put one's overall moral stance into question.

Sometimes it is argued that what is objectionable about racial preference is that "the extension of a right or benefit to a minority [has] the effect of depriving persons who were not members of a minority group of benefits which they would otherwise have enjoyed."[25] Yet other transfers of benefits of this sort that have more impact on people's lives than diversity affirmative action are often regarded as justified under U.S. law. Consider:

1) Using open immigration laws to benefit businesses by providing them with low-wage labor while decreasing the economic opportunities of the less skilled residents of our inner cities;
2) Keeping the unemployment rate high to fight inflation, which benefits businesses by restricting the job opportunities of the unemployed;
3) Keeping inheritance tax relatively low, which benefits the wealthy at the expense of the poor who would tend to benefit from greater public revenue.

Although these policies, like diversity affirmative action, clearly transfer benefits from some to others, few publicly object to any of these policies. Could the difference be that these policies generally transfer benefits from the less advantaged to the more advantaged? Surely that couldn't be an acceptable reason for favoring these policies over diversity affirmative action!

Regardless, the opponents of diversity affirmative action have to show why such transfers of benefits are justified while those required by affirmative action are not, and it does not seem that they can do so.[26]

Of course, there are nonminority males holding desirable positions in society who have benefited more from past discrimination than have the nonminority males who would lose out to women or minority affirmative action candidates. Ideally, an affirmative action program should be demanding sacrifices from these well-positioned nonminority males as well. This could be done by requiring them to retire early, or by allowing diversity affirmative action considerations to take precedence over seniority rules when layoffs become necessary.[27] Maybe we could target, among others, nonminority male college professors who have taught for more than twenty years. Yet while it would be morally preferable to place the burdens of diversity affirmative action on those who have benefited most from past discrimination, when that is not politically feasible, it would still be morally permissible to place the burden primarily on nonminority males who are competing for jobs and positions with diversity affirmative action candidates, given that they have benefited from past discrimination, although not as much as others.[28]

Carl Cohen also attacks diversity affirmative action programs in higher education, wrongly treating them as if they were remedial affirmative action programs when they clearly are not. For example, Cohen claims that "a daughter of a black physician who graduates from a fine college has been done no injury entitling her to preferential consideration in competitive admissions."[29] But even if this were true (and Cohen offers no evidence to show that even middle class blacks in the United States do not suffer, among other things, from white privilege[30]), the claim is simply irrelevant to a critique of diversity affirmative action. Diversity affirmative action does not purport to be justified on the backward-looking grounds that its recipients have suffered from present or past discrimination. Rather, it purports to be justified on the forward-looking grounds that its recipients can provide diversity, and this is surely something that middle-class blacks who graduate from fine colleges can succeed in doing.

Of course, the ability of affirmative action candidates to provide diversity is not unconnected to present and past discrimination. Usually, it is because underrepresented minorities have experienced the effects of present or past discrimination themselves, which enables them to bring diversity into educational contexts, and this is true even of middle-class minorities.[31] Still, the justification for diversity affirmative is not any compensation that its recipients might receive for present or past discrimination they suffered, but rather the diversity that they bring to the student body from which all can benefit.

Nevertheless, Cohen does raise an appropriate objection to nonremedial affirmative action programs that seek to provide diversity. He challenges such programs for failing to treat people as equals. The benefits of diversity, Cohen claims, cannot override our obligation to treat people as equals. To support his claim, Cohen asks us to suppose that segregated classrooms significantly improved learning and teaching. If we think that such educational benefits cannot justify the inequalities of segregated classrooms, Cohen argues, then we should also think that the educational benefits of diversity cannot justify departing from our obligation to treat people as equals.[32]

Yet while Cohen's comparison of segregated and diverse classrooms is appropriate here, his argument fails. This is because the problem with racially segregated classrooms is that they do not significantly improve learning and teaching for all students. Separate but equal simply does not work for all students. If, for some inexplicable reason, everyone happened to do just fine under a segregated equal educational system (a claim that is sometimes made in support of sex segregated schools) then there would no longer be any objection it. Thus, the argument against racial segregation is based on its negative effects, particularly for those who are less advantaged. We reject racial segregation because of its negative effects, and we endorse diversity in education because of its positive effects.[33] Though Cohen's comparison between segregated and diverse classrooms is surely appropriate here, the differences in their effects require that we evaluate them differently.

Moreover, if using racial preference for the sake of diversity violates our obligation to treat everyone as equals, then so would the use of athletic, veterans', and legacy preferences, as well as of the many laws in the United States that favor the rich and the middle class over the poor. In our book, Cohen says nothing explicitly about these other "preferences," except to claim that racial preferences "have most corrupted admissions in recent years," which could imply that they are much more morally objectionable than either legacy or athletic preferences.[34] Cohen provides no argument for this assertion.

I have claimed that we need an argument that compares racial preferences with the other forms of preference. Clearly, these forms of preference
have a greater impact on college admissions, and are arguably less justified than racial preferences. The same holds true for many legally established preferences that favor the rich and the middle class over the poor,
such as anti-inflation fiscal policies and low inheritance taxes. If we want
to treat everyone as equals, we would certainly have to focus our critique
on legacy and athletic preferences and other legally established preferences
that favor the rich and the middle class over the poor, rather than focus, as
Cohen does, on critiquing racial preferences.

Recently, a number of colleges and universities (such as Kenyon College, Pepperdine University, Santa Clara University, and The College of
William and Mary) have begun engaging in another form of diversity
affirmative action—affirmative action for men—now that 57 percent of
U.S. college students are female according to a 2008 NBC poll.[35] Surely, it
would be very odd for colleges and universities to use this form of affirmative action while rejecting race-based affirmative action.

Third Objection

Diversity affirmative action has been criticized for being illegal, in violation of the Civil Rights Act of 1964, and for being unconstitutional, in violation of the Fourteenth Amendment.

Clearly, the Civil Rights Act does prohibit racial preferences that exclude or discriminate, but it cannot preclude, as noted earlier, those racial
preferences or classifications that are needed for its very enforcement. In
addition, the Supreme Court has also consistently interpreted the Act not
to preclude the use of racial preferences in other contexts; for example, as
a means for providing diversity in an educational context. Here again, the
Civil Rights Act has to be taken as prohibiting not all racial preferences,
but only illegitimate ones.

Now the constitutional justification of diversity affirmative action depends on its purported benefits, and critics have challenged those benefits. For example, Cohen claims that efforts to show that racial diversity
in educational institutions has important benefits have failed to do so.[36]
He cites the National Association of Scholars' study of Patricia Gurin's

Expert Report in *Gratz v. Bollinger,* which claims that her own data disconfirms that campus racial diversity is correlated with educational excellence. However, in raising this point, Cohen neither sets out Gurin's argument nor considers her response to the critique of her work by the National Association of Scholars.

Gurin had argued that the racial and ethnic composition of the student body are positively correlated to classroom diversity and having informal discussions of race or close friends of a different race, which in turn are correlated with positive learning and democracy outcomes (e.g., more active thinking processes and citizen engagement). In their critique, the authors of the National Association of Scholars' study speculated that if Gurin's data were subject to a regressive analysis, it would yield no correlation between the racial and ethnic composition of student bodies, positive learning, and democracy outcomes. In her response, Gurin claims that this speculation is correct, but it in no way adversely affects her argument.[37] To use another example, if we were to do a regressive analysis on damage to lung tissue in a study of smoking and lung cancer, we should expect that there would be no correlation between smoking and lung cancer. In the smoking/lung cancer case, the effect that is controlled for (i.e., damage to lung tissue) is the very mechanism by which smoking has its cancerous effect. Likewise, in Gurin's study, taking diversity courses and having informal discussions of race or close friends of a different race are the very mechanisms by which racial and ethnic composition of student bodies has its positive learning and democracy outcomes.[38] If we controlled for these mechanisms, then, of course, we will not get the same positive outcomes from diversity affirmative action. Hence, this failed critique of Gurin's report provides no support for Cohen's constitutional attack on diversity affirmative action.[39]

Cohen also quotes from the abstract of another study, which sought to establish that diversity does *not* improve university education.[40] Unfortunately, Cohen does not tell us how the authors got to their conclusion; he just appeals to their authority.[41] The authors of this study used data from a random sample to determine whether the satisfaction of students with their college or university experience was positively correlated with the level of diversity at the college or university they attended. The authors of this study found that it was not. In fact, they found that, to some degree, it was negatively correlated.

As it turns out, this study makes the same mistake at a practical level that the authors of the National Association of Scholars study had made theoretically in their attempt to criticize Gurin's Expert Report in *Gratz v. Bollinger*. The authors of the National Association of Scholars's study had *speculated* that if Gurin's data were subject to a regressive analysis that controlled for taking diversity courses and having informal discussions of race or close friends of a different race, it would yield no correlation at all between the racial and ethnic composition of student bodies and positive learning and democracy outcomes.

This study does not simply *speculate* what would be the result of controlling for the mechanisms by which the racial and ethnic composition of student bodies has positive educational outcomes. It goes further and carries out a study that does control for these mechanisms by ignoring them and compares the racial and ethnic diversity with positive educational outcomes. Not surprisingly, as Gurin would have predicted, the study shows that racial and ethnic diversity and certain positive educational outcomes are not correlated. Yet to get a positive correlation, according to Gurin, colleges and universities must have in place the diversity courses and informal discussions of race that serve to translate racial and ethnic diversity into positive educational outcomes. Thus, this study that Cohen cites, like earlier studies, does not support Cohen's constitutional attack on diversity affirmative action. Cohen himself develops no other argument against this form of affirmative action.[42]

It is worth pointing out here in *Gratz v. Bollinger* (2001) both sides had agreed to a summary judgment acknowledging that there was no disagreement of fact between them, only a disagreement of law. Specifically, during the course of the trial, the counsel for the plaintiffs conceded that diversity at the University of Michigan was "good, important and valuable." It was only after they had lost this case at the district court level, that the counsel for the plaintiffs introduced the critique of the National Association of Scholars as an amicus curiae brief to challenge Gurin's report. We have seen that this study and two other related studies are fundamentally flawed in what they try to establish.[43] But it also should be mentioned that to introduce the study at the point in the legal proceedings is an impermissible move for the plaintiffs to make because it attempts to supplement the factual record on appeal and sidestep the rigors of cross-examination that assure the integrity of facts found at the district court level.

9

Affirmative Action
around the World

In his 2004 book, *Affirmative Action Around the World,* Thomas Sowell argues that not only are the consequences of affirmative action bad for the United States, but also that a study of affirmative action in other countries suggests that things could get worse for the United States if it pursues its misguided policy.

More specifically, Sowell summarizes what he thinks we can learn from viewing affirmative action around the world:

> Preceding chapters have shown, time and again, intergroup violence arising from majority groups that no one has discriminated against, and preferences and quotas being given to such groups, whose only real problem has been their inability to compete with more skilled and more diligent minorities.[1]

And, by and large, this is what we learn from a study of affirmative action in Malaysia, Sri Lanka, Nigeria, and certain states of India. In Malaysia, the politically dominant native Malays voted for employment and educational preferences for themselves over ethnic Chinese who had emigrated to Malaysia during its recent colonial period and, without discriminating against anyone, had generally become better educated and more prosperous than the native Malays. In Sri Lanka, the politically dominant Sinhalese enacted preferences for themselves over the Tamil minority, who, without discriminating against anyone, had generally become better educated and more prosperous than the Sinhalese. This led to a civil war, which has yet to be fully resolved. In Nigeria, the politically dominant Hausa-Fulani tribes of the northern region voted in employment and educational preferences for themselves over the Ibo tribe of the southern region, whose members had benefited more during the recent colonial period in terms of education and government employment. This conflict in Nigeria led the southern region to attempt to succeed and form the separate state of Biafra. A civil war put an end to the secessionist attempt but without resolving the underlying political conflict. In India, particularly in the states of Assam and Maharashtra, native political majorities have enacted preferences for themselves over outsiders who had outperformed them in the marketplace or in examinations for college admissions or government jobs. These preferential actions have also been accompanied by violent outbursts between the contending parties.

Given the history of affirmative action in these countries, it is difficult to generalize from its practice to the practice of affirmative action in the United States. Nevertheless, Sowell tries to make the different practices look similar. He suggests that just as those who enacted and benefited from affirmative action in each of these countries constitute a majority, the same has been true in the United States once affirmative action was extended to women.[2] But even this similarity hides a stark difference. The type of affirmative action that most women have benefited from in the United States is outreach—the form that Sowell himself endorses. This form of affirmative action simply requires employers to check out the available women candidates before making their hiring or admission decisions. It does not involve any change in the usual standards for hiring and admission. This is quite different from the ethnic majority-based affirmative action found in the countries that Sowell surveys.

Despite these striking differences, there are some similarities between affirmative action for blacks in the United States and for untouchables in India, which is a national not a state-based program. In both countries, the benefits of affirmative action do not usually go to the most disadvantaged members of the preferred groups. In India, positions that are reserved for untouchables require complementary resources to make use of them, and the poorest of the untouchables do not have such resources. Consequently, only the more advantaged among the untouchables have been able to benefit from these preferences.

In the United States, those minorities who are able to benefit from diversity affirmative action tend to have certain advantages that other minorities lack; they are not the least advantaged members of their groups. The explanation for this is that in neither country are these affirmative action programs designed to help the truly least advantaged members of minority groups. Rather they are designed to benefit minorities who already have certain advantages, and, in the case of the United States, they are designed to benefit nonminorities as well.

Nevertheless, this limitation of the affirmative action programs is not necessarily an objection to them. If one wants to replace them with a well-funded program that does help the least advantaged in society, for example, my proposed $25 billion a year equal education opportunity program, I am sure that every defender of diversity affirmative action would favor the change, assuming that it was not possible to have both programs. However, the political reality in both India and the United States is that either we retain these affirmative action programs with all their limitations or we have nothing at all. When faced with such a choice, surely affirmative action programs deserve our support.

Sowell is clearly worried that history will repeat itself.[3] Given the horrendous failures of affirmative action programs in Malaysia, Sri Lanka, Nigeria, and certain states of India, Sowell is concerned that a comparable failure is in store for the United States. But there are significant differences between the ethnic majority-based programs in these other countries and the ethnic minority-based one in the United States. Moreover, while the affirmative action program in India for untouchables does parallel in some ways affirmative action for blacks in the United States, the limitations of both programs are traceable to the unwillingness of the respective political majorities to do more for those who are truly least advantaged. Supporters of affirmative action in both countries would surely favor more extensive programs if they were politically feasible. The problem is that they are not. At the moment, affirmative action in the United States happens to be the best we can get.

In sum, Sowell's attempt to compare the practice of affirmative action in other countries to that in the United States fails because of fundamental differences between the ethnic majority-based programs in other countries and the ethnic minority-based one in the United States. Moreover, while there are similarities between affirmative action programs in India for untouchables and affirmative action in the United States, for blacks, these similarities do not undercut support for either program.

Conclusion

Following the U.S. Civil War, there was a flurry of legal activity that attempted to remedy the injustices of slavery. The withdrawal of federal troops from the South in 1877, together with new oppressive state laws and supportive Supreme Court decisions, however, ushered in a period of Jim Crow laws, culminating in the Supreme Court's separate but equal decision of *Plessy v. Ferguson* (1896). It was not until the *Brown v. Board of Education* decisions in 1954 and 1955, the Civil Rights Acts of 1964 and 1972, and a number of Supreme Court decisions on affirmative action—*Griggs* (1971), *Bakke* (1978), *Fullilove* (1980), and *Local 28 of the Sheetmetal Workers' International* (1986)—that the United States started to move toward greater enforcement of racial justice.

Yet, starting the late 1980s, there has been a trend to interpret the Equal Protection Clause of the Fourteenth Amendment in such a way that it primarily protects the white majority in this country against minority claims to compensation for present and past discrimination. This trend can be found in the Supreme Court decisions in *Croson* (1989) and *Adarand* (1995), in the

U.S. Court of Appeals for Fifth Circuit decision in *Hopwood* (1996), and California's Proposition 209 (1996). The *Grutter v. Bollinger* decision (2003) was a welcomed respite from this trend. However, opponents of affirmative action have now returned to using referendums, as with the Michigan Civil Rights Initiative, to frame the issue in terms of racial preferences rather than affirmative action and the benefits of diversity, thereby undercutting the *Grutter* decision, at the same time that more and more colleges and universities are beginning to engage in affirmative action for men![1]

In the end, opponents of affirmative action seem to be in the grip of an odd notion of racial equality. They seem unconcerned with the kind of evidence I cited in chapter 1 about widespread existing discrimination against minorities and women. They do not call for increasing the meager efforts of the federal government to prosecute this sort of discrimination. Nor are they interested in overturning the Supreme Court decisions that make it very difficult to prove or correct discrimination against minorities. Moreover, they are generally not in favor of the large increases in spending that are needed to provide all students in the United States with at least a K through 12 quality education. Rather, they are focused particularly on eliminating such programs as diversity affirmative action, which benefit underrepresented minorities by benefiting the student body as a whole. This selective concern with eliminating certain benefits to minorities is far too narrow and inadequate an ideal of racial equality if it is that. We need to do better. In this book, I have argued that we should support the following requirement for *outreach affirmative action:*

> All reasonable steps must be taken to ensure that qualified minority, women, and economically disadvantaged candidates are made as aware of existing jobs and positions that are available to them as are nonminority, male, or economically advantaged candidates.

I have also argued for the following requirements as to when *remedial affirmative action* is justified:

> 1) The past discrimination that is to be remedied must be proven discrimination, but the institution that is engaging in the affirmative action need not be implicated in that proven discrimination in order for the affirmative action in question to be justified.

2) Although, in a colorblind (racially just) society, racial classifications would no longer be presumptively suspect, in the United States, racial classifications must be regarded as presumptively suspect because of the 250 years of slavery, 100 years of Jim Crow laws, plus discriminatory practices that continue right up to the present day. However, the standard of proof required to justify the use of racial classifications in remedial affirmative action should not be unreasonably high as it was in the *Croson* case. It should not be easier to correct for sexual discrimination in society than it is to correct for racial discrimination. Accordingly, remedial affirmative action still has a significant role in combating proven past and present discrimination in housing, education, and jobs, unless more broadly conceived and much better funded corrective policies to more directly remedy these injustices are undertaken.

3) Only candidates are selected whose qualifications are such that when their selection is combined with a suitably designed educational enhancement program, they will normally turn out, within a reasonably short time, to be as qualified as, or even more qualified than, their peers.

4) Those who are passed over by such affirmative action programs would have been found to have benefited from the discrimination suffered by the affirmative action candidates, for example, the discrimination found in their unequal educational and residential opportunities.[2]

Last, I have argued that we should regard *diversity affirmative action* as justified when the following requirements are met:

1) Race is used as a factor to select from the pool of applicants a sufficient number of qualified applicants to secure the educational benefits that flow from a racially and ethnically diverse student body.

2) Preference is given to economically disadvantaged applicants by cutting legacy and other preferences for the rich and relatively rich at elite colleges and universities.

3) Only candidates are selected whose qualifications are such that when their selection is combined with a suitably designed educational enhancement program, they will normally turn out, within a reasonably short time, to be as qualified as, or even more qualified than, their peers.

Only by implementing these requirements will we be able to reach that colorblind (racially just), gender-free (sexually just), and equal opportunity (economically just) society to which both defenders and critics of affirmative action claim to aspire.

NOTES

Introduction

1. *Grutter v. Bollinger,* 539 U.S. (2003).

2. Presumably, the reason O'Connor thought that race-based affirmative action would no longer be needed once her educational requirement had been met is that then, through the regular admission process, minorities would no longer be underrepresented in higher education. Diversity would be secured in that way.

3. Terence Pell, "The Nature of Claims about Race and the Debate over Racial Preferences," *International Journal of Applied Philosophy* 18 (2004): 23.

4. Outreach affirmative action discussed in chapter 4 is different. It is rarely contested, although recently there has been an attempt to limit it.

5. With the exception of outreach affirmative action under some, possibly restricted, interpretation.

6. A corollary of this approach is to have the government stop gathering data on racial and sexual disparities in society, which, of course would make it difficult to assess the degree to which people are suffering from racial and sexual discrimination. Ward Connerly tried, but failed, to get a referendum (Prop. 54) in California passed to that effect in 2003.

1. Current Racial and Sexual Discrimination

1. Mitchell Chang, Daria Witt, James Jones, and Kenji Hakuta, *Compelling Interest* (Stanford: Stanford University Press, 2003), 98.

2. Maria Krysan, "Recent Trends in Racial Attitudes" (2002), http://tigger.cc.uic.edu.

3. Jamillah Moor, *Race and College Admissions* (Jefferson, NC: McFarland, 2005), 200.

4. Jody David Armour, "Hype and Reality in Affirmative Action," *University of Colorado Law Review* 68 (1997): 1173.

5. Ibid.

6. Howard Schuman, Charlotte Steeh, Lawrence Bobo, and Maria Krysan, *Racial Attitudes in America: Trends and Interpretations,* rev. ed. (Cambridge: Harvard University Press, 1997). Virtually the same percentage of whites continued to hold this view from 1962 through 2002. See http://tigger.cc.uic.edu/~krysan/writeup.htm.

7. Derrick Bell, *Silent Covenants* (New York: Oxford University Press, 2004), 96.

8. See Michael Brown et al., *White-Washing Race* (Berkeley: University of California Press, 2005), chapters 2 and 5; Todd Michael Furman, "A Dialogue Concerning Claim Jumping and Compensatory Justice," *Teaching Philosophy* 21 (1998): 131–51: Deborah Jones. "The Future of Bakke: Will Social Science Matter?" *Ohio State Law Journal* 59 (1998): 1054–67; Gerald Jaynes and Robin Williams, eds., *A Common Destiny* (Washington, DC: National Academy Press, 1989); Andrew Hacker, *Two Nations* (New York: Ballantine Books, 1992); Gertrude Ezorsky, *Racism and Justice* (Ithaca: Cornell University Press, 1991); *Hunger 1995: Fifth Annual Report on the State of World Hunger* (Silver Spring, MD: Bread for the World Institute, 1995).

9. Judy Lichtman et al., "Why Women Need Affirmative Action," in *The Affirmative Action Debate,* ed. George Curry, 175–83 (Reading, MA: Perseus Books, 1996).

10. Leonard Steinhorn and Barbara Diggs-Brown, *By the Color of Our Skin* (New York: Dutton, 1999), 47.

11. Tom L. Beauchamp, "Goals and Quotas in Hiring and Promotion," in *Ethical Theory and Business* by Tom L. Beauchamp and Norman Bowie, 5th ed., 379ff (Upper Saddle River, NJ: Prentice-Hall, 1996).

12. Bryan Grapes, ed., *Affirmative Action* (San Diego: Greenhaven Press, 2000), Introduction.

13. Ibid.

14. Ibid.

15. M. V. Lee Badgett, *Economic Perspectives on Affirmative Action* (Washington, DC: Joint Center for Political and Economic Studies, 1995), 5.

16. LeAnn Lodder et al., *Racial Preference and Suburban Employment Opportunities* (Chicago: Legal Assistance Foundation and the Chicago Urban League, April 2003).

17. Devah Pager and Bruce Western, "Race at Work: Realities of Race and Criminal Record in the New York City Job Market" (2005), http://www.nyc.gov/html/cchr/pdf/race_report_web.pdf; Salim Muwakkil, "Have We Put Racism behind Us? Don't Kid Yourselves," *Wall Street Journal,* September 29, 2003.

18. The Impact Fund, Berkeley, California, www.impactfund.org.

19. Richard Tomasson et al., *Affirmative Action* (Washington, DC: American University Press, 1996).

20. T. Hsien and F. H. Wu, "Beyond the Model Minority Myth," in *Affirmative Action Debate,* ed. G. E. Curry (Cambridge, MA: Perseus, 1998).

21. Claude S. Fischer et al., *Inequality by Design* (Princeton: Princeton University Press, 1996), 164–65.

22. S. G. Stolberg, "Race Gap Seen in Health Care of Equally Insured Patients," *New York Times,* March 21, 2002.

23. Faye Crosby, *Affirmative Action Is Dead; Long Live Affirmative Action* (New Haven: Yale University Press, 2004), 200.

24. Muwakkil, "Have We Put Racism behind Us?"

25. Ibid.

26. Steven R. Donziger, *The Real War on Crime* (New York: HarperCollins, 1999), 99.

27. "Five Reasons to Oppose the Death Penalty," Campaign to End the Death Penalty (pamphlet, 2006), http://nodeath.server269.com/downloads/583fivereasons.pdf.

28. Marcia Coyle, "When Movements Coalesce," *National Law Journal,* September 21, 1992. See also B. J. Goldman, *Not Just Prosperity: Achieving Sustainability with Environmental Justice* (Washington, DC: National Wildlife Federation, 1993.)

29. Coyle, "When Movements Coalesce."

30. Ibid.

31. Coyle, "When Movements Coalesce."

32. Ibid.

33. Ibid.

34. For a summary and a critique of Farrell's views, see Warren Farrell and James P. Sterba, *Does Feminism Discriminate Against Men?—A Debate* (New York: Oxford University Press, 2008).

35. Jean-Marie Navetta, "Gains in Learning, Gaps in Earning," *AAUW Outlook* (Spring 2005): 12.

36. Joan Williams, *Unbending Gender: Why Family and Work Conflict and What to Do About It* (New York: Oxford University Press, 2000), 274.

37. Tom L Beauchamp. "In Defense of Affirmative Action," *Journal of Ethics* 2 (1998): 143–58.

38. Lichtman, "Why Women Need Affirmative Action."

39. Ibid.

40. Ibid.

41. Cherly Gomez-Preston, *When No Means No* (New York: Carol, 1993), 35–36. The problem is international as well as national. A three-year study of women in Estonia, Finland, Sweden, and the Soviet Union showed that nearly 50 percent of all working women experience sexual harassment. A survey released in 1991 by the Santama Group to Consider Sexual Harassment at Work showed that about 70 percent of Japanese women say they have experienced some type of sexual harassment on the job. See Teresa Webb, *Step Forward* (New York: Master Media, 1991), xiv, xvii.

42. Ellen Bravo and Ellen Cassedy, *The 9–5 Guide to Combating Sexual Harassment* (New York: John Wiley, 1992), 4–5.

43. Gomez-Preston, *When No Means No.*

44. Ibid.

45. *New York Times,* November 11, 1996 and February 4, 1997.

46. Linda Bird Francke, *Ground Zero* (New York: Simon & Shuster, 1997), 157.

47. Diana Schemo, "Rate of Rape at Academy Is Put at 12 Percent in Survey," *New York Times,* August 29, 2003.

48. U.S. Department of Defense, "Armed Forces Survey 2002 Sexual Harassment Survey," Defense Technical Information Center, Ft. Belfort, Virginia. In 2002 the Department of Defense excluded "unwanted sexual behavior" as part of the measure for sexual harassment, which reduced the frequency of sexual harassment in 1995 to 45 percent and to 24 percent in 2002. But why was unwanted sexual behavior removed from the measure of sexual harassment? The 2002 survey provides no explanation for this change. Could it have been done to just reduce the overall figure for sexual harassment?

49. Evelyn Murphy with E. J. Graff, *Getting Even* (New York: Simon & Shuster, 2005), 90–91.

50. Londa Schiebinger, "Women's Health and Clinical Trials," *Journal of Clinical Investigations* 112 (2003): 973–77.

51. Londa Schiebinger, *Has Feminism Changed Science* (Cambridge: Harvard University Press, 2001), 113–25.

52. Ibid.

53. Ibid.

54. Ibid.

55. Sue Rosser, *Women's Health—Missing from U.S. Medicine* (Bloomington: Indiana University Press, 1994), 22.

56. Stella Hurtley and John Benditt, "Women's Health Research," *Science* 269 (August 1995): 777.

57. Rosser, *Women's Health,* 11.

58. For a discussion of the data on discrimination against women, see Farrell and Sterba, *Does Feminism Discriminate against Men,* 127–235.

2. A Legal History of Race- and Sex-Based Affirmative Action

1. The phrase was first used in the 1935 National Labor Relations Act. There it meant that an employer who was found to be discriminating against union members or union organizers would have to stop and take affirmative action to place those victims where they would not be subjected to discrimination. For a fuller account of the relevant history, see John Skrentny, *The Ironies of Affirmative Action* (Chicago: University of Chicago Press, 1996); Barbara Bergmann, *In Defense of Affirmative Action* (New York: Basic Books, 1996); Robert J. Weiss, *We Want Jobs* (New York: Garland, 1997); Eric Schnapper, "Affirmative Action and the Legislative History of the Fourteenth Amendment," *Virginia Law Review* 71 (1985): 753–98.

2. Ibid.

3. Skrentny, *The Ironies of Affirmative Action,* 123.

4. Ibid., 124.

5. Ibid., 169–70.

6. Bergmann, *In Defense of Affirmative Action,* 173.

7. Ibid., 169–70.

8. *Contractors Association of Eastern Pennsylvania v. Secretary of Labor,* 311 F. Supp. 1002, 1009 (E.D. Pa 1970).

9. Bergmann, *In Defense of Affirmative Action,* 52.

10. One amendment prohibited "discrimination in reverse by employing persons of a particular race…, in either fixed or variable numbers, proportions, percentages, quotas, goals or ranges." The other made Title VII's prohibition of preferential treatment applicable to executive orders. Both were voted down (22 to 44 and 30 to 60, respectively).

11. Bergmann, *In Defense of Affirmative Action,* 54.

12. Weiss, *We Want Jobs,* 189.

13. Ibid., 192.

14. See Martha Burk, "Time to Bury Reagan's Legacy for Women" (June 11, 2004), http://www.womensnews.org/article.cfm/dyn/aid/1866.

15. Skrentny, *The Ironies of Affirmative Action,* 227.

16. The decisions struck down with respect to the need for strict scrutiny when dealing with racial classifications were *Fullilove v. Klutznick* (1980) and *Metro Broadcasting v. Federal Communications Commission* (1990).

17. Thomas Espenshade and Chang Chung, "The Opportunity Costs of Admission Preferences at Elite Universities," *Social Science Quarterly* 86 (2005): 293–305.

18. Actually the legal jurisdiction of the *Hopwood* decision by the U.S. Court of Appeals for the Fifth Circuit included Texas, Louisiana, and Mississippi, but its legal effect is only being felt in Texas because Louisiana and Mississippi are still under court orders to desegregate their public universities.

19. It rose to 1.8 percent (9 students) in 1998, and fell to 1.7 percent (9 students) in 1999.

20. It increased to 1 percent (5 students) in 1998 but fell to 0.4 percent (2 students) in 1999.

21. It increased to 7.6 percent (37 students) in 1998 and to 8.1 percent (42 students) in 1999.

22. In 1998, a similar amendment was passed in the state of Washington (Initiative 200).

23. Tyche Hendricks, "UC Minority Admissions Rebound, but Berkeley Lags," *San Francisco Chronicle,* April 4, 2001.

24. In 1998 the African American enrollment at Berkeley was 8, in 1999 it fell to 7, in 2000 it remained at 7, and in 2001 it rose to 14.

25. Carol Allen, *Ending Racial Preferences: The Michigan Story* (Lanham, MD: Lexington Books, 2008), chapter 2.

26. One United Michigan (http://oneunitedmichigan.org) and Allen, *Ending Racial Preferences,* chapters 2 and 3.

27. Allen, *Ending Racial Preferences,* 61ff.

28. Allen, *Ending Racial Preferences,* chapters 2 and 5.

29. Susan Kaufmann, "The Gender Impact of the Proposed Michigan Civil Rights Initiative," Center for the Education of Women, University of Michigan (revised January, 2006), 7.

30. Allen, *Ending Racial Preferences,* 73ff.

31. Robert J. Birgeneau, "Anti-Bias Law Has Backfired at Berkeley," *Los Angeles Times,* March 27, 2005.

32. David Leonhardt, "The New Affirmative Action," *New York Times Magazine,* September 20, 2007, 78. Leonhardt recounts in this article a successful attempt to increase the number of incoming blacks at UCLA in 2007, but suggests that this may have been done by violating the law.

33. William Allen, quoted in Allen, *Ending Racial Preferences,* 244. In one of his responses to questions, William Allen does come up with a case where I think everyone would grant the person involved is harmed by affirmative action. Allen imagines Clarence Thomas, or maybe someone like him (maybe Allen himself), being criticized for opposing affirmative action after clearly having benefited from it. Obviously, it is very difficult for Thomas, or anyone like him, to argue against this criticism. Would Thomas (or Allen) be maintaining that although he has clearly benefited from affirmative action, others will not similarly benefit, or at least most others will not? If so, it is very difficult to argue for this view especially if there doesn't seem to be anything especially unique about oneself or one's own situation. If one really wants to argue against the beneficial effects of affirmative action, one clearly is at a disadvantage if one has actually benefited from it oneself. And being so disadvantaged could also count as a way of being harmed. Of course, this sort of case wouldn't show that affirmative action was unjustified but that in a certain way one had been harmed (disadvantaged) by having benefited from it given what one now wants to argue. See Allen, *Ending Racial Preferences,* 225.

Nevertheless, someone receiving affirmative action could surely be better off without it, that is, could be better off if there were no such system. Such a person might be so talented, he or she would still have been very successful, given that the person's success would not have been attributed to affirmative action. But this case too would not show that affirmative action is unjustified. If it did, a similar argument could be raised against veterans' preference. Surely, the success of some veterans, e.g., after World War II, would have been greater if people did not think of them as veterans' preference recipients. Yet no one should think that this undercuts the justification for veterans' preference.

34. Looked at in another way, in 2004, UCLA and Berkeley produced the most and the third most applicants to law schools in the country. The University of California at Riverside was the 114th ranked feeder institution for law schools, sending only one-seventh as many applicants as UCLA. Cherly Harris and William Kidder, "The Black Student Mismatch Myth in Legal Education" (2004), http://www.equaljusticesociety.org/Sander_Harris_Kidder_JBHE_Article_2_05.pdf, p. 102.

35. Allen, *Ending Racial Preferences,* chapter 3; Leadership Conference on Civil Rights, Memorandum, January 30, 2007.

36. Operation King's Dream, 2006 U.S. Dist. Lexis 61323.

37. Ibid.

38. Ibid.

39. Ibid.

40. Report of the Michigan Civil Rights Commission Regarding the Use of Fraud and Deception in the Collection of Signatures for the Michigan Civil Rights Initiative Ballot Petition (June 7, 2006).

41. *Operation King's Dream v. Connerly* Case No. 06-12773.

42. For further discussion, see Jocelyn Benson, "Election Fraud and the Initiative Process: A Study of the Michigan Civil Rights Initiative," *Fordham Urban Law Review* 34 (April 2007): 889.

43. The U.S. Congress approved warrantless wiretapping and electronic surveillance by the government in July 2008 even before the Inspector General's report assessing the utility of these measures had been issued.

3. How Best to Define Affirmative Action

1. In 2001 the Supreme Court has ruled that Congress does not have the authority to require states to ensure that the handicapped have certain (access) rights. See *Board of Trustees of the University of Alabama v. Patricia Garrett.*

2. Cohen attributes this same conception of affirmative action to me in our co-authored book, *Affirmative Action and Racial Preference—A Debate* (New York: Oxford University Press, 2003). Cohen writes, "Sterba defends *naked* preference, preferences awarded to all the members of certain ethnic groups, merely in virtue of their membership" (295; emphasis in original). After repeated requests extending over several years to indicate where in our co-authored book I endorse such a view, Cohen finally responded that he could not cite any passage in my text where I endorse the view, but that this is the view of affirmative action that I must be endorsing, given that I defend racial preferences (email correspondence, April 23, 2007). Nothing could be farther from the truth. My definition indicates how only certain, and not all, members of ethnic groups can be appropriate recipients of affirmative action, and then only when specific normative conditions are satisfied. Or to phrase it another way, as I have argued repeatedly in this book, we all, Cohen included, defend racial preferences. It is just a question of when and where.

3. Critics need to target the most morally defensible form of affirmative action if they really want to show that however it is characterized, affirmative action is morally objectionable. In other words, critics need to address their strongest opponents.

4. I have also proposed a definition, which allows that particular affirmative action programs can be justified or not dependent on how well or ill they instantiate the goals of affirmative action.

5. Note also that what I defend is not captured by what Louis Pojman calls strong affirmative action. Yet, it should also be noted that Pojman combines his opposition to affirmative action with support of a range of more radical welfare and environmental programs, which I too support, but, which, unlike affirmative action, are politically unfeasible at the present time. See, in particular, Pojman's "Straw Man or Straw Theory: A Reply to Mosley," *International Journal of Applied Philosophy* 12 (1998): 169–80, and "Pedaling Power: Sustainable Transportation," in his *Environmental Ethics,* 3rd ed., 549–51 (Belmont, CA: Wadsworth, 2001).

6. I am not using "minority" here to refer to someone who is not white. For the purposes of affirmative action, whites can count as minorities, as whites who lived in Michigan's Upper Peninsula did in the university's affirmative action program.

7. For further discussion of the ideal of gender-free society, which I also call an androgynous society, see my books *Justice for Here and Now* (New York: Cambridge University Press, 1998) and *Three Challenges to Ethics* (New York: Oxford University Press, 2001).

8. Affirmative action, as I conceive of it, has equal opportunity as one of its ultimate goals, but only insofar as that goal can be attained though economic justice (not by means of a broader social and economic justice).

9. Mark Weber, "West Germany's Holocaust Payoff to Israel and World Jewry," *The Journal of Historical Review* (1988): 243–50.

10. Matt Kelley, "Congress Approves $23 Million Settlement for Tribe," *Associated Press,* October 17, 2000.

11. James Stedman, "Federal Pell Grant Program of the Higher Education Act," Report for Congress, Domestic Science Division, March 18, 2003.

12. See Carl Cohen, "Why Race Preference Is Wrong" in Cohen and Sterba, *Affirmative Action and Racial Preference,* chapter 6, p. 77.

13. Another way to think about what defenders and critics of affirmative action are disagreeing about is to recognize that neither side is opposed to legitimate racial and sexual preferences, such as when an actor who is African American is chosen to play Othello or a woman doctor is selected to work in a rape crisis center. Rather, what they disagree about is the nature and extent of illegitimate racial and sexual preferences.

14. I am defining affirmative action for a context where the benefits of diversity can serve the ultimate goal of racial justice rather than just being compatible with it as would obtain in a racially just society.

15. One might wonder how diversity affirmative action candidates could be the most qualified, given that, as I argue later, they may still need remedial help for a certain period of time. The reason this is the case is that the qualifications that affirmative action candidates lack can be remedied, whereas the qualification that nonaffirmative action candidates clearly lack—diversity— usually cannot be remedied. It is in this sense that nonaffirmative action candidates are not the most qualified.

4. A Defense of Outreach Affirmative Action

1. Thomas Sowell, *Affirmative Action Reconsidered* (Washington, DC: American Enterprise Institute for Public Policy Research, 1975), 3. Likewise, Supreme Court Justice Clarence Thomas at his confirmation hearings spoke passionately of his support for outreach affirmative action.

2. Kathryn M. Neckerman and Joleen Kirschenman, "Hiring Strategies, Racial Bias and Inner-City Workers," *Social Problems* 38 (1991): 433, 437–41.

3. Ibid., 440.

4. Ibid., 438.

5. Gertrude Ezorsky, *Racism and Justice: The Case for Affirmative Action* (Ithaca: Cornell University Press, 1991), 15.

5. A Defense of Remedial Affirmative Action

1. Tom Beauchamp, "In Defense of Affirmative Action," *Journal of Ethics* 2 (1998): 143–58.

2. Ibid.

3. Steve Watkins, *The Black O: Racism and Redemption in an American Corporate Empire* (Athens: University of Georgia Press, 1997). The title of this book derives from the company's practice, not found in any corporate manual, of color-coding minority job applications by blackening the "O" in Shoney's to make sure they were passed over for certain jobs.

4. *Haynes et al. v. Shoney's Inc.* U.S. District 749 (N.D. Fla. Jan. 25, 1993).

5. Steve Watkins, *The Black O: Racism and Redemption in an American Corporate Empire* (Athens: University of Georgia Press, 1997), 228.

6. Kurt Eichenwald, "Texaco Executives, On Tape, Discuss Impeding Bias Suit," *New York Times,* November 4, 1996.

7. Ibid.

8. Ibid. Note there was also a dispute about exactly which belittling remarks were recorded on the tape. See Kurt Eichenwald, "Investigation Finds no Evidence of Slur on Texaco Tapes," *New York Times,* November 11, 1996.

9. "Judge Approves Texaco Settlement," *Legal Intelligencer,* March 27, 1996.

10. Ibid.

11. Ibid.

12. Alison Frankel, "Tale of the Tapes," *American Lawyer* (March, 1997); *New York Times,* November 4, 1996. "Texaco Chairman Says Company Bias Is 'Tip of the Iceberg' in Corporate America," *Jet,* December 16, 1996, 5(1).

13. Greg Winter, "Coca-Cola Settles Racial Bias Case," *New York Times,* November 17, 2000.

14. Ibid.

15. This sort of remedial affirmative action was also mandated by other parts of the AT&T, Shoney's, Texaco, and Coca-Cola settlements.

16. *Local 28 of the Sheetmetal Workers Union v. EEOC* 478 U.S. 421 (1986).

17. Robert Weiss, *We Want Jobs* (New York: Garland Publishers, 1997), 99–100.

18. Given that at the time only some fraction of minorities who had satisfactorily completed apprenticeship programs were admitted into New York craft unions, it was reasonable to admit minorities into the Local 28's apprenticeship program at the higher rate of 1:1 if one hoped to have minorities admitted into the union in proportion to their availability in the local labor pool. In fact, of 600 minorities who successfully completed other union training programs in New York City some years before this Supreme Court case was decided, only 40 actually received union books. See ibid., 215.

19. I think that it is possible to interpret or justify some earlier court decisions in the same way that I have done with this court case. In *Contractors Association of Eastern Pennsylvania v. the Secretary of Labor* (1973), which dealt with the Philadelphia Plan, the federal court was concerned with a five-county Philadelphia area where minorities made up 30 percent of all construction workers but only 1 percent of the workers in six craft unions. The federal government's Philadelphia Plan conditioned the granting of federal construction money upon accepting a set of goals and timetables for improving minority apprenticeship or membership with respect to these unions. The Court found the Philadelphia Plan to be an acceptable way of increasing equal opportunity for minorities in the Philadelphia area. In *United Steelworkers of America v. Weber* (1979) the factual situation was quite similar. Blacks represented 39 percent of the local population in Gramercy, Louisiana but only 2 percent of the craftworkers and 15 percent of the unskilled workers at the plant, up from 10 percent in 1969 when the company began to hire unskilled workers at the gate on a "one white, one black" basis. However, the company continued the practice of hiring skilled craft workers, from virtually all-white craft unions outside the Gramercy area, which accounted for the small percentage of minorities in craft positions at the plant. Under pressure from the federal government, Kaiser Aluminum and the unions agreed to jointly manage a craft apprenticeship program that would accept one minority worker and one white worker from two different seniority lists until the percentage of minority workers approximated the percentage of minorities in the Gramercy area. Since neither Kaiser Aluminum nor the unions nor Weber, who brought suit against the apprenticeship program, was interested in justifying the program as a means for putting an end to discrimination at the Gramercy plant, the case was argued and decided on other grounds. But it could have been argued and decided on grounds similar to those that were used in the cases from New York City and Philadelphia.

20. *EEOC v. AT&T* 365 F. Supp. 1105 (1973).

21. *Local 28 of the Sheetmetal Workers Union v. EEOC* 478 U.S. 421 (1986).

22. Barbara Bergmann, *In Defense of Affirmative Action* (New York: Basic Books, 1996), 32–61.

23. Ibid., 56–57.

24. See Thomas Sowell's *Civil Rights: Rhetoric or Reality?* (New York: William Morrow, 1984), *Preferential Politics: An International Perspective* (New York: William Morrow, 1990), and *Race and Culture* (New York: Basic Books, 1994).

25. There is evidence that Asian Americans tend to be concentrated at the extremes, both at the high and low ends of social status indicators, and that even when they are successful, they still

tend to experience a "glass ceiling" that limits their success. See Deborah Woo, *Glass Ceilings and Asian Americans* (Lanham, MD: Rowman & Littlefield, 2000).

26. *City of Richmond v. J.A. Croson Co.* (1987), 501. The Court held this opinion even as it rejected a particular affirmative action program as unconstitutional.

27. Sowell, *Affirmative Action Around the World,* 182.

28. Exploring statistical disparities are also the grist of criminal investigations. If a woman took out a large insurance policy on her husband just a month before he died from food poisoning, this "statistical disparity" is most likely to make her a primary suspect in the case, until contrary evidence becomes available.

29. Of course, sometimes statistical disparities, even between whites and blacks, provide no evidence at all of discrimination as in the high proportion of African Americans in the National Basketball Association and in other professional sports. Fortunately, professional sports is one area where talent, or the lack of it, is easily manifest. Moreover, given the general favoritism enjoyed by whites in U.S. society, surely no professional team in the United States is going to prefer a clearly less talented African American player over a more talented white player.

30. Weiss, *We Want Jobs,* 3.

31. Of course, if we lived in a colorblind society, racial classifications would no longer be presumptively suspect because in such a society a person's race would be no more significant than eye color. For further development of this idea, see Richard Wasserstrom, "Racism, Sexism and Preferential Treatment," *UCLA Law Review* 24 (1977): 581–622. In most societies, people frequently don't even notice a person's eye color. Except for the mildest aesthetic preferences, eye color tends to be an unimportant trait. Very little turns on what eye color you have. Accordingly, if we lived in a society where a person's race was no more significant than eye color is in most societies, there would be little reason to treat race with any kind of legal scrutiny. In a colorblind society, many cultural differences would remain, but they wouldn't be based on race. As a result, the cultures that were constituted by these differences would be open to members of all races in much the same way that most religions today are open to members of all races.

Obviously we don't live in such a colorblind, or, if you prefer, racially just society. In the United States, it is not difficult to find present discrimination as well as the continuing effects of past discrimination.

32. For a fuller discussion of this comparison, see Edwin Hettinger, "What Is Wrong with Reverse Discrimination?" *Business & Professional Ethics Journal* 6 (1987): 39–55.

33. There are some instances where remedial affirmative action has been successful. For example, there was the approval of compensation to black farmers in *Pigford v. Glickman* (D.D.C., 1999). See also Ken Cook, "How a Widening Farm Subsidy Gap Is Leaving Black Farmers Further Behind," *Environmental Working Group,* July 2007.

34. On this point, see Lawrence Thomas, *Vessels of Evil: American Slavery and the Holocaust* (Philadelphia: Temple University Press, 1992).

35. See Paul Wellstone and Jonathan Kozol, "What Tests Can't Fix," *New York Times,* March 13, 2001; Gary Orfield and John Yun, "Resegregation in American Schools," The Civil Rights Project, Harvard University, 1999; Gary Orfield, "The Resegregation of Our Nation's School," *Civil Rights Journal* (Fall 1999): 8–13; William Celis, "Study Finds Rising Concentration of Blacks and Hispanic Students," *New York Times,* December 14, 1993; Micaela di Leonardo, "White Lies, Black Myths," *Voice,* September 22, 1992.

36. Before the creation of the FHA, mortgages generally were granted for no more than two-thirds of the appraised value of a home, and frequently banks required half the assessed value of a home before making a loan. The FHA, by contrast, required only a 10 percent downpayment, and it extended the repayment period to twenty-five to thirty years, thus resulting in low monthly payments. Consequently, many more families were able to purchase homes than would otherwise have been possible.

37. Before 1900, blacks and whites usually lived side by side in American cities. In the North, the small native black population was scattered widely throughout white neighborhoods. Even Chicago, Detroit, and Philadelphia, cities that are now known for their large black ghettos, were not segregated. In southern cities such as Charleston, New Orleans, and Savannah, black servants and laborers lived on alleys and side streets near the mansions of their white employers.

38. In this respect, the ineffectiveness of the Fair Housing Act of 1968 parallels the ineffectiveness of the Civil Rights Act of 1964, after which it was modeled.

39. According to one survey, although 88 percent of white respondents agreed that black people should have a right to live wherever they can afford to, only 43 percent would feel comfortable in a neighborhood that was one-third black. According to another survey, although 57 percent of white respondents felt that white people did not have a right to discriminate against black people, only 35 percent would vote for a law that would ensure that a homeowner could not refuse to sell to someone because of his or her race.

40. Peter Schmidt, *Color and Money* (New York: Palgrave Macmillan, 2007), 47.

41. If these were our options, it may turn out that some critics would favor retaining affirmative action over such a radical equal educational opportunity alternative. But defenders would not favor retaining affirmative action if these were the options.

42. Michael Brown et al., *White-Washing Race* (Berkeley: University of California Press, 2005), chapter 4.

43. If someone passed over by an affirmative action program could make the case that he or she had not benefited from the discrimination suffered by the relevant affirmative action candidates (something it would be very difficult to do in the United States given its level of racial and sexual discrimination) that would have to be taken into account.

44. The question arises as to how we might implement such an affirmative action program. Clearly there are ways to do so. At Georgia Tech, the performance gap between white and minority first-year engineering students was eliminated by instituting an intensive five-week summer course for the minority students. See Susan Strom and Lani Guiner, "The Future of Affirmative Action: The Innovative Ideal," *California Law Review* 84 (1996): 10.

45. If someone passed over by an affirmative action program could make the case that he or she had not benefited from the discrimination suffered by the relevant affirmative action candidates (something it would be very difficult to do in the United States given its level of racial and sexual discrimination) that would have to be taken into account.

6. Objections to Remedial Affirmative Action

1. Christopher Morris, "Existential Limits to the Rectification of Past Wrongs," *American Philosophical Quarterly* 21 (1984): 175–82.

2. A few African Americans, particularly those who have come or whose ancestors have come from the Caribbean, are not the product of slavery in the United States, but almost all African Americans have slavery in their background.

3. A similar example was used by James Woodward in "The Non-Identity Problem," *Ethics* 96 (1986): 804–31. Woodward also provides the example of Viktor Frankl who suggests that his imprisonment in a Nazi concentration camp enabled him to develop "certain resources of character, insights into the human condition and capacities for appreciation" that he would not otherwise have had. At the same time, we clearly want to say that the Nazis unjustifiably violating Frankl's rights by so imprisoning him. Woodward, p. 809. See also Norman Daniels, "Intergenerational Justice," (2003), http://plato.stanford.edu/entries/justice-intergenerational.

4. Carl Cohen, "Should Federal Affirmative Action Programs Continue?" *Congressional Digest* (June–July 1996): 185.

5. *City of Richmond v. J. A. Croson Co.* (1987), at 501.

6. Cohen, "Should Federal Affirmative Action Programs Continue?" 183, 185.

7. For the argument that blacks as a group deserve affirmative action, see Paul Taylor, "Reserve Discrimination and Compensatory Justice," *Analysis* 33 (1973): 177–82; Michael Bayles, "Reparations to Wrong Groups," *Analysis* 33 (1973): 182–84; and Albert Mosley and Nicholas Capaldi, *Affirmative Action: Social Justice or Unfair Preference?* (Lanham, MD: Rowman & Littlefield, 1996), chapter 1. For the argument, that they don't, see George Sher, *Approximate Justice* (Lanham, MD: Rowman & Littlefield, 1997), chapters 1–8.

8. This argument can be expressed as follows:

1) The discrimination practiced in the Shoney's Restaurant chain ought to be stopped and compensation paid.
2) The proposed financial settlement and reassignments are an appropriate means for stopping and compensating for that discrimination.
3) An affirmative action program employing just those means ought to be implemented.

9. The arguments in these examples can be expressed as follows:

a) A discriminatory practice ought to be stopped.
b) A particular program will effectively put an end to that practice.
c) An affirmative action program employing just those means ought to be implemented.

x) Those who have suffered from past discrimination ought to receive compensation.
y) Each of the members of a particular racial group in a particular context has suffered from past discrimination.
z) An affirmative action program that compensates the members of that racial group ought to be implemented.

10. For example, we might envision someone arguing for affirmative action from the premise that people ought to be compensated simply because they belong to a group many of whom have suffered from discrimination. But while Cohen would surely reject such a premise, so would most defenders of remedial affirmative action.

11. It is here that there are grounds for complaint about college and university admission procedures, and it is here that the overwhelming number of admission slots is at stake. Yet, surprisingly there is little complaint about the continuing use of these flawed standards for the greater majority of admission slots. It is as if the powers to be in this context are content that admission to elite schools should highly correlate with nothing more than family income.

12. James Fishkin, *Justice, Equal Opportunity, and the Family* (New Haven: Yale University Press, 1983), 88, 89, 105.

13. Although blacks do not deserve compensation because they are black, that is, because they belong to the group of black individuals, it sometimes seems that blacks are discriminated against simply because they are black, that is, simply because they belong to the group of black individuals. But on closer analysis, it would appear that blacks are not discriminated against simply because they are black but because those doing the discriminating unjustifiably believe that blacks are lazy or unclean or something similar. For this and other related points, see James Nickel, "Should Reparations Be to Individuals or Groups?" *Analysis* 34 (1974): 154–60.

14. See Carl Cohen, *Naked Racial Preference* (Boston: Madison Books, 1995): 107–9.

7. A Defense of Diversity Affirmative Action

1. The University of Texas Law School, like most state law schools, does "discriminate" against nonresidents; it reserves 80 percent of its seats for Texas residences.

2. For a discussion of this point, see Reva Siegel, "The Racial Rhetorics of Colorblind Constitutionalism: The Case of Hopwood v. Texas," in *Race and Representation: Affirmative Action,* ed. Robert Post and Michael Rogin, 29–72 (New York: Zone Books, 1998).

3. Patricia Gurin, "The Compelling Need for Diversity in Higher Education," *Gratz v Bollinger,* no. 97-75231 (E.D. Mich.) (2000). For additional evidence, see Thomas Weisskoff, "Consequences of Affirmative Action in U.S. Higher Education: A Review of Recent Empirical Studies," *Economic and Political Weekly,* December 22, 2001.

4. These factors included sixteen points for being from the Upper Peninsula of Michigan.

5. Even if we were to grant that the Brennan group did not even implicitly endorse diversity as an acceptable grounds for taking race into account in higher education, preferring instead the grounds that it corrects for past discrimination, it would still follow that Powell's opinion is the holding in *Bakke.* This is because, according to the Supreme Court's decision in *Marks v. United States* (1977), "the holding of the Court may be viewed as that position taken by those members who concurred in the judgment on the narrowest grounds." Clearly, Powell and the Brennan group concur in using race as a factor in higher education. Moreover, Powell's diversity grounds are narrower than the Brennan's group's grounds of correcting for past discrimination in the sense that it is less controversial. (In *Marks* the narrowest grounds is understood to be least controversial grounds.) So even if we assume that the Brennan group did not even implicitly endorse the diversity rationale, Powell's decision should be taken to be holding in the *Bakke* case.

6. In *Johnson v. Board of Regents of the University of Georgia* (2001), the U.S. Court of Appeals for Eleventh Circuit struck down the University's affirmative action program on the grounds that its pursuit of diversity was not sufficiently narrowly tailored. The Court of Appeals allowed that the University of Georgia (UG) had used seven factors to measure diversity in 1999, and had added two more—economic disadvantage and academic disadvantage—for 2000, but the Court still argued that this was not enough to be narrowly tailored. According to the Court, what the UG needed to do was include even more factors for achieving diversity and to read and qualitatively evaluate each applicant's file—something the university did for fewer than 1,000 of the 13,000 or so applicants each year. Typically, the UG admitted 85 percent of its students based on their academic indexes and SAT scores alone. Seemingly, then, what the Court is proposing is that if the UG wishes to use race as factor in the pursuit of diversity then it would have to do a file-by-file evaluation of all applicants because only then could it know what kind of diversity each applicant could provide irrespective of his or her academic index and SAT scores. Of course, if the university were to just drop race as a factor from its pursuit of diversity (or substitute, say, left-handedness), it could proceed as before with no objection from the Court. It is only because the UG with 6 percent black students in a state that is nearly 30 percent black had sought to maintain or slightly increase its enrollment of minority students that the Court seeks to impose these more stringent requirements, far beyond any requirements that Powell in the *Bakke* decision had envisioned.

7. "Brief of Amicus Curiae, The Michigan Association of Scholars in Support of Petitioners," http://www.vpcomm.umich.edu/admissions/legal/gru_amicus-ussc/mas_both.pdf, p. 5.

8. This is not always the case. Thomas Wood and Malcolm Sherman seem to imagine whites taking ethnic studies courses in which no blacks or Latinos were present and benefiting just as much as they would have if minorities had been present. Unfortunately, they do not explain how this could happen. See their report "Race and Higher Education" (National Association of Scholars, May 2001), http://www.nas.org/polReports.cfm?Doc_Id=89, p. 86.

9. See Eric Schnapper, "Affirmative Action and the Legislative History of the Fourteenth Amendment," *Virginia Law Review* 71 (1985): 753–98.

10. Unfortunately, with the end of Reconstruction, the rise of the Ku Klux Klan, and Jim Crow laws in the South, appeals to the Fourteenth Amendment ceased, as the United States entered a period of almost 100 years of blatant racial segregation that was not all that different from the 200 years of slavery that preceded it.

11. Before the interment policy, there was no evidence of Japanese Americans spying for Japan, although there was evidence of German Americans spying for Germany. In the *Korematsu* decision, either the Supreme Court failed to apply its own criterion or the criterion was viewed as fairly easy to meet. How else would the internment of Japanese Americans been viewed as necessary for the security of the United States?

12. They do not establish that diversity is not an important enough goal because they do not show that the consequences of operating without racial preferences are virtually always better than the consequences of having used them.

13. The majority in *Grutter* granted a certain deference to the Law School with respect to its judgment concerning the educational importance of diversity. (I would do the same, although I wouldn't ground my decision on the First Amendment as the Court tries to do.)

14. Terence J. Pell, "Racial Preferences and Formal Equality," *Journal of Social Philosophy* 34 (2003): 309–25. This article was presented in the first of two public debates that Pell and I had on affirmative action, one before and one after the *Gratz* and *Grutter* decisions.

15. Even the due process requirements in the criminal justice are end-state-driven requirements. Their goal is to convict and punish only those who are actually guilty of the crimes with which they are charged.

16. Establishing whether or not there is an important enough state purpose to justify the use of racial preferences/classifications is one part of that consequentialist evaluation.

17. Although the Florida Plan seems more generous than the Texas Plan, appearances are deceiving. The Florida Plan does not guarantee admission to the state's two flagship universities—University of Florida and Florida State University, whereas the Texas Plan guarantees admission to its two flagship universities—University of Texas and Texas A&M University.

18. There may be a slight difference here in that these plans may have been adopted *both* to produce a racial result and a geographical result.

19. Ronald Roach, "Tricky Times for the Top 10% Program," *Diverse Online* (August 9, 2007), http://www.diverseeducation.com/artman/publish/article_9014.shtml.

20. Richard Kahlenberg, *The Remedy: Class, Race, and Affirmative Action* (New York: Basic Books, 1997); Richard Kahlenberg, "In Search of Fairness: A Better Way," *Washington Monthly* (June 1998): 26–30.

21. Claude Steele and Joshua Aronson, "Stereotype Threat and the Intellectual Text Performance of African Americans," *Journal of Personality and Social Psychology* 69 (1995): 797–811.

22. See my response to the third objection in chapter 6, where I similarly claim that simply being a member of a particular racial group is not grounds for receiving remedial affirmative action.

23. Or more accurately, the factor is being discriminated against because the discriminator unjustifiably believes that all the members of the minority group or all women are inferior for some reason or other, and so treats them in a discriminatory way.

24. There is another objection to Michigan Law School's diversity affirmative action program, forcefully stated by Chief Justice Rehnquist in his dissent. Rehnquist is implicitly arguing that other means are preferable because there is something objectionable about the means chosen by Michigan Law School. He points out that the Law School admitted African American applicants in roughly the same proportion to their number in the applicant pool as Hispanic and American Indian applicants, even though some African American applicants had GPAs and test scores that were lower than some of the Hispanic applicants who were rejected. Given that the Law School was looking for a critical mass of each underrepresented group, Rehnquist finds the rejection of the Hispanic applicants hard to explain, particularly because the Law School admits twice as many African Americans as Hispanics, and only one-sixth as many American Indians. How could the Law School be admitting a critical mass of each group?

The Law School, however, never claimed to be admitting a critical mass of each group. It was only aiming at that goal, and clearly it was far from reaching it with respect to American Indians.

In addition, there surely are other relevant factors, such as the qualify of essays and of letters of recommendation, that could explain why some African Americans with lower grade and test scores were admitted while some Hispanic applicants with higher grade and test scores were rejected. The objection that Rehnquist raises here had not been raised before. Nor was it raised in the oral argument before the Supreme Court. So it is not clear exactly how the Law School would respond. Still, a response of the sort that I have just now sketched surely looks like it would support the Law School's admissions process in this regard. One might also argue that the University of Michigan Law School had more of a legitimate regional interest in admitting African American candidates, while, say, the University of Arizona Law School would have more of a legitimate regional interest in admitting American Indian or Latino candidates.

25. Walter Benn Michaels, *The Trouble with Diversity* (New York: Metropolitan Books, 2006), 86.

26. Peter Schmidt, *Color and Money* (New York: Palgrave Macmillan, 2007), 17.

27. Ibid., 18.

28. David Golden, *The Price of Admission* (New York: Crown Publishers, 2006), 287.

29. Schmidt, *Color and Money,* 4.

30. Golden, *The Price of Admission,* 5–6.

31. Schmidt, *Color and Money,* 31.

32. Golden, *The Price of Admission,* 131.

33. Ibid.

34. Ibid., 7.

35. Ibid., 125.

36. Except from the seven sister colleges, there were very few alumna graduates from elite colleges in the United States at the time.

37. Golden, *The Price of Admission.*

8. Objections to Diversity Affirmative Action

1. Charles Murray, "Affirmative Racism," in James P. Sterba, *Morality in Practice,* 6th ed., 251–57 (Belmont: Wadsworth, 2000).

2. In the example cited from Murray, the black woman appears to lack the qualifications so that even "a suitably designed educational enhancement program" would not have resulted in her becoming, within a reasonably short time, as qualified as or even more qualified than their peers. For that reason, affirmative action was not justified in this case.

3. Thomas Sowell, *Affirmative Action Around the World* (New Haven: Yale Univerity Press, 2004), 145–46.

4. Derek Bok and Willam Bowen, *The Shape of the River* (Princeton: Princeton University Press, 1998), 61 and 259.

5. Sowell, *Affirmative Action Around the World,* 146–47.

6. William Boden and Derek Bok, "Access to Success," *ABA Journal* (February 1999): 62–63, 67.

7. Richard Sander, "A Systemic Analysis of Affirmative Action at American Law Schools," *Stanford Law Review* 57 (2004): 367.

8. Ibid.

9. See David Chambers et al., "The Real Impact of Eliminating Affirmative Action in American Law Schools," *Stanford Law Review* 57 (2005): 1855. Ian Ayers and Richard Brooks, "Does Affirmative Action Reduce the Number of Black Lawyers?" *Stanford Law Review* 57 (2005): 1807.

10. Richard Sander, "A Reply to Critics," *Stanford Law Review* 57 (2005): 1963.

11. Sander, "A Systemic Analysis of Affirmative Action at American Law Schools," 483.

12. Chambers et al., "The Real Impact of Eliminating Affirmative Action in American Law Schools," p. 1896, n. 145.

13. Richard Lempert et al., "Affirmative Action in American Law Schools: A Critical Response to Richard Sander's 'Reply to Critics,'" University of Michigan Law School Olin Center Working Paper No. 60, available at http://papers.ssrn.com/sol3/papers.cfm?abstract_id=886382 (February 2006).

14. Sander, "A Systemic Analysis of Affirmative Action at American Law Schools," 437, table 5.5.

15. Sander, "A Reply to Critics," 1995.

16. See Chambers et al., "The Real Impact of Eliminating Affirmative Action in American Law Schools," and Ian Ayers and Richard Brooks, "Does Affirmative Action Reduce the Number of Black Lawyers?"

17. Ibid.

18. Ayers and Brooks, "Does Affirmative Action Reduce the Number of Black Lawyers?"

19. Ibid., 1996.

20. Barry Gross, "The Case Against Reverse Discrimination," in James P. Sterba, *Morality in Practice,* 4th ed., 250–60 (Belmont: Wadsworth, 1994).

21. I suppose someone could reject both programs on the grounds that they both show preferences for women and minorities, although Program B lacks most of those features to which critics of affirmative action object. However, the critic who persisted in this way would need an argument for rejecting these particular sorts of preferences given that we know that simply rejecting all racial and sexual preferences would be illegitimate.

22. Do the benefits to those who gain from a reliance on standardized tests like the SAT and the LSAT outweigh the losses to those who lose out from that reliance?

23. Most public professional schools significantly favor in-state applicants. For example, the three public medical schools in West Virginia limit out-of-state applicants to 10 percent of their first-year classes.

24. John Skrentny, *The Ironies of Affirmative Action* (Chicago: University of Chicago Press, 1996).

25. The Supreme Court of California, *Regents of the University of California v. Bakke* (1976).

26. If one thinks that these transfers are also objectionable, why then should not these transfers, rather than the transfers involved with racial preferences, be the first to be eliminated?

27. For a discussion of this issue, see Gertrude Ezorsky, *Racism and Justice: The Case for Affirmative Action* (Ithaca: Cornell University Press, 1991). Interestingly, veteran's preference, but not racial preference, has been understood to trump seniority rules.

28. In order to distribute the burdens of affirmative action programs more fairly, public revenues could be used, where appropriate, to defray the costs of whatever educational or training programs are required for implementing such programs.

29. Carl Cohen and James P. Sterba, *Affirmative Action and Racial Preference* (New York: Oxford University Press, 2003), chapter 4, 32.

30. White privilege is an unearned privilege all whites have, but rarely notice, which puts nonwhites at a disadvantage. Some examples include:

1) Whites can go shopping alone most of the time, assured that they will not be followed or harassed.

2) Whites can use checks, credit cards, or cash, and can count on their skin color not to work against the appearance of financial reliability.

3) Whites can arrange to protect their children most of the time from people who do not like them.

4) Whites can do well in a challenging situation without being called a credit to their race.

5) Whites are never asked to speak for all the people of their racial group.

6) If a traffic cop pulls whites over or if the IRS audits their tax returns, they can be sure they haven't been singled out because of their race.

7) Whites can be pretty sure that if they ask to talk to the "person in charge" they will be facing a person of their race.

Many more examples can be found in Peggy McIntosh, "White Privilege: Unpacking the Invisible Knapsack," http://seamonkey.ed.asu.edu/~mcisaac/emc598ge/Unpacking.html. As one commentator has put it, "the only real disadvantage to being white is that it so often prevents people from understanding racial issues." See also Sylvia Law, "White Privilege and Affirmative Action," *Akron Law Review* 32 (1999) 603–27.

31. Patricia Gurin gives the following example of how middle-class blacks can aid the understanding of minority perspectives in a classroom setting. She reports:

In one class session, a white woman student who had grown up in a homogeneously white town in Michigan expressed, with considerable emotion, that she was tired of being categorized as white. "I'm just an individual. No one knows if I hold similar beliefs to those of other white students just by looking at me. I hate being seen just as white." She ended in tears. An African-American male student who had grown up in a virtually all white city in Connecticut replied as he walked toward her across the classroom. "I just want to be an individual also. But every day as I walk across this campus—just as I am walking across this room right now—I am categorized. No one knows what my thoughts are, or if my thoughts align with other African- American students. They just see me as a black male. And at night, they often change their pace to stay away from me. The point is—groups do matter. They matter in my life and (as he approached the other student whose hand he then took), they matter in your life." There was silence in the room.

Gurin further comments, "The students learned about the meaning of groups and the meaning of individuals in a way that they won't soon forget." See Patricia Gurin, "Response to the Critique by the National Association of Scholars of the Expert Witness Report of Patricia Gurin in *Gratz v. Bollinger* and *Grutter v. Bollinger,*" Available at http://umich.edu/admissions/new/gurin/html.Similarly, in *Grutter v. Bollinger,* U.S. Court of Appears for Sixth Circuit (2002), Justice Clay maintains, "Notwithstanding the fact that the black applicant may be similarly situated financially to the affluent white candidates, this black candidate may very well bring to the student body experiences rich in the African-American traditions emulating the struggle the black race has endured in order for the black applicant even to have the opportunities and privileges to learn." Justice Clay also notes, "A well dressed black woman of wealthy means shopping at Neiman Marcus or in an affluent shopping center may very well be treated with the same suspect eye and bigotry as the poorly dressed black women of limited means shopping at Target."

32. Cohen and Sterba, *Affirmative Action and Racial Preference,* 23–40.

33. On this point see Bernard Boxill, *Blacks and Social Justice,* rev. ed. (Lanham, MD: Rowman and Littlefield, 1992), chapters 4–6, especially 146.

34. Ibid., chapter 8, 157.

35. Jenny Fedor, "Affirmative Action…for Men?" *U-Wire,* March 20, 2008, http://phoenix.swarthmore.edu/2008/03/20/news/affirmative-action-for-men; Scott Jaschik, "Affirmative Action for Men," *Inside Higher Ed,* March 27, 2006, http://www.insidehighered.com/news/2006/03/27/admit; and Peter Hong, "A Growing Gender Gap Tests College Admissions," *Los Angeles Times,* November 21, 2004.

36. Cohen and Sterba, *Affirmative Action and Racial Preference,* 91ff.

37. Ibid.

38. Gurin provides the following report from one student of how taking a diversity course affected her:

The most helpful aspect of the course was reading the articles from so many different perspectives and then discussing them with so many different kinds of students in the class. Living through the heated discussions in class and being asked to participate actually rocked my world. I realize that my past pattern of not talking in class and being invisible was a way of avoiding having to think about or engage in difficult and complex issues. Now that I have engaged and even disagreed with others, it seems like there is no turning back. I'm ready now to wrestle with ideas and multiple perspectives. This change has spilled over into other areas of my life also. I actually am doing much better in my other classes because I am not afraid to think, speak, and be challenged intellectually. The racial and ethnic diversity in this class did this for me. This finally feels like what college is supposed to be about.

See "Supplemental Expert Report of Patricia Gurin, *Grutter v. Bollinger,*" January 11, 2001.

39. Cohen mentions a 2001 study—"A Critique of the Expert Report of Patricia Gurnin," by Robert Lerner and Althea Nagai, done for the Center for Equal Opportunity, Washington, DC— that was critical of the Gurin Report. Cohen, however, does not mention Gurin's response to this study in which she argues that it fails in much the same way as the study by the National Association of Scholars's study fails.

40. Stanley Rothman, Seymour Martin Lipset, and Neil Nevitte, "Does Enrollment Diversity Improve University Education?" *International Journal of Opinion Research* (forthcoming).

41. Cohen and Sterba, *Affirmative Action and Racial Preference,* 92, note 124.

42. It is interesting to note that just a few years ago, Cohen defended Justice Powell's opinion in *Bakke* (1979) on the constitutional permissibility of diversity affirmative action. See his *Naked Racial Preference* (Boston: Madison Books, 1995), chapter 3. Nor has Cohen been misled by what we now see is the failed attack of the National Association of Scholars on Patricia Gurin's empirical defense of diversity affirmative action. Rather his current view is that diversity affirmative action would not be justified even if it produced beneficial results because it fails to treat all citizens as equals in the way that the U.S. Constitution requires (see ibid., chapter 6, 102 and note 38). Here Cohen again ignores the comparative question of how we can constitutionally oppose this form of "preference" while justifying other forms of preference, most of which are more sweeping in their effects on people's lives. It seems like a good idea to interpret the U.S. Constitution so that it does not encourage or permit gross forms of injustice.

43. One of these two related studies is discussed in the text, the other in note 39 above.

9. Affirmative Action around the World

1. Thomas Sowell, *Affirmative Action Around the World: An Empirical Study* (New Haven: Yale University Press, 2004), 183.

2. Ibid., 11.

3. Ibid., 166.

Conclusion

1. Surprising, some of the most ardent opponents of race-based affirmative action seem unusually tolerant of affirmative action for men. For example, Terrence Pell, president of the Center for Individual Rights, finds the practice perfectly legal as long as it is not carried too far. See, Peter Hong, "A Growing Gender Gap Tests College Admissions, *Los Angeles Times,* November 21, 2004.

2. If someone passed over by an affirmative action program could make the case that he or she had not benefited from the discrimination suffered by the relevant candidates (something that would be very difficult to do in the United States given its level of racial and sexual discrimination) that would have to be taken into account.

BIBLIOGRAPHY

Books and Articles

Allen, Carol. *Ending Racial Preferences: The Michigan Story.* Lanham, MD: Lexington Books, 2008.

Ayers, Ian, and Richard Brooks. "Does Affirmative Action Reduce the Number of Black Lawyers?" *Stanford Law Review* 57 (2005): 1807.

Badgett, M. V. Lee. *Economic Perspectives on Affirmative Action.* Washington, DC: Joint Center for Political and Economic Studies, 1995.

Baylis, Michael. "Reparations to Wrong Groups." *Analysis* 33 (1975): 182–84.

Beauchamp, Tom L. "In Defense of Affirmative Action." *Journal of Ethics* 2 (1998): 143–58.

Bell, Derrick. *Silent Covenants.* New York: Oxford University Press, 2004.

Benson, Jocelyn. "Election Fraud and the Initiative Process: A Study of the Michigan Civil Rights Initiative." *Fordham Urban Law Review* 34 (April 2007): 889.

Bergmann, Barbara. *In Defense of Affirmative Action.* New York: Basic Books, 1996.

Birgeneau, Robert J. "Anti-Bias Law Has Backfired at Berkeley." *Los Angeles Times,* March 27, 2005.

Bowen, William, and Derek Bok. *The Shape of the River: Long-Term Consequences of Considering Race in College and University Admissions.* Princeton: Princeton University Press, 1998.

Boxill, Bernard. *Blacks and Social Justice.* Totowa, NJ: Rowman & Allanheld, 1984.

———. "The Case for Affirmative Action." In *Morality in Practice,* edited by James P. Sterba, 260–72, 4th ed. Belmont, CA: Wadsworth, 1994.

Brown, Michael, et al. *White-Washing Race.* Berkeley: University of California Press, 2005.

Cahn, Steven, ed. *Affirmative Action and the University.* Philadelphia: Temple University Press, 1993.

Chambers, David, et al. "The Real Impact of Eliminating Affirmative Action in American Law Schools." *Stanford Law Review* 57 (2005).

Chang, Mitchell, et al. *Compelling Interest.* Stanford, CA: Stanford University Press, 2003.

Clayton, Susan, and Faye Crosby. *Justice, Gender, and Affirmative Action.* Ann Arbor: University of Michigan Press, 1992.

Cohen, Carl. *Naked Racial Preference.* Boston: Madison Books, 1995.

———. "Should Federal Affirmative Action Programs Continue?" *Congressional Digest* (June–July, 1996).

———. "Preference by Race in University Admissions and the Quest for Diversity." *Journal of Urban and Contemporary Law* 54 (1998): 43–72.

Cohen, Carl, and James P. Sterba. *Affirmative Action and Racial Preference—A Debate.* New York: Oxford University Press, 2003.

Crosby, Faye. *Affirmative Action Is Dead; Long Live Affirmative Action.* New Haven: Yale University Press, 2004.

Curry, George, ed. *The Affirmative Action Debate.* Reading, MA: Perseus Books, 1996.

De Zwart, Frank. "The Logic of Affirmative Action: Caste, Class and Quotas in India." *Acta Sociologica* 43 (2000): 235–49.

D'Souza, Dinesh. *The End of Racism.* New York: Free Press, 1995.

Dyer, Holly. "Gender-Based Affirmative Action: Where Does It Fit in the Tiered Scheme of Equal Protection Scrutiny?" *University of Kansas Law Review* 41 (1993): 591–613.

Eastland, Terry. *Ending Affirmative Action: The Case for Colorblind Justice.* New York: Basic Books, 1996.

Epstein, Cynthia. "Affirmative Action." *Dissent* (Fall 1995): 463–65.

Epstein, Richard. *Forbidden Grounds: The Case Against Employment Discrimination Laws.* Cambridge, MA: Harvard University Press, 1992.

Espenshade, Thomas, and Chang Chung. "The Opportunity Costs of Admission Preferences at Elite Universities." *Social Science Quarterly* 86 (2005): 293–305.

Ezorsky, Gertrude. *Racism and Justice: The Case for Affirmative Action.* Ithaca: Cornell University Press, 1991.

Fish, Stanley. "Reverse Racism, or How the Pot Got to Call the Kettle Black." *Atlantic Monthly* (November 1993), http://www.theatlantic.com/doc/199311/reverse-racism.

Fishkin, James. *Justice, Equal Opportunity, and the Family.* New Haven: Yale University Press, 1983.

Forbath, William, and Gerald Torres. "The Talented Tenth." *Nation,* December 15, 1997.

Furman, Todd Michael. "A Dialogue Concerning Claim Jumping and Compensatory Justice." *Teaching Philosophy* 21 (1998): 131–51.

Golden, David. *The Price of Admission.* New York: Crown Publishers, 2006.

Grapes, Bryan, ed. *Affirmative Action.* San Diego: Greenhaven Press, 2000.

Gross, Barry. "The Case against Reverse Discrimination." In *Morality in Practice,* edited by James P. Sterba, 255–60, 4th. ed. (Belmont, CA: Wadsworth, 1994).

Guinier, Lani. "The Real Bias in Higher Education." *New York Times,* June 24, 1997.

Gurin, Patricia. "The Compelling Need for Diversity in Higher Education." *Gratz v Bollinger,* no. 97-75231 (E.D. Mich.) (2000).

Gutmann, Amy, and Kwame Appiah. *Color Conscious: The Political Morality of Race.* Princeton: Princeton University Press, 1996.

Hacker, Andrew. *Two Nations.* New York: Ballantine Books, 1992.

Hettinger, Edwin. "What Is Wrong with Reverse Discrimination?" *Business & Professional Ethics Journal* 6 (1987): 39–55.

Kahlenberg, Richard. "Class, not Race." *New Republic* (April 3, 1995): 21–26.

——. *The Remedy: Class, Race, and Affirmative Action.* New York: Basic Books, 1997.

——. "In Search of Fairness: A Better Way." *Washington Post,* June 1998, 26–30.

Kaufmann, Susan. "The Gender Impact of the Proposed Michigan Civil Rights Initiative." The Center for the Education of Women, University of Michigan, revised (January 2006).

Lempert, Richard, et al. "Affirmative Action in American Law Schools: A Critical Response to Richard Sander's 'Reply to Critics.'" University of Michigan Law School Olin Center Working Paper No. 60, available at http://papers.ssrn.com/sol3/papers.cfm?abstract_id=886382 (February 2006).

Leonhardt, David. "The New Affirmative Action." *New York Times Magazine,* September 20, 2007.

Lodder, LeAnn, et al. *Racial Preference and Suburban Employment Opportunities.* Chicago: Legal Assistance Foundation and the Chicago Urban League, April 2003.

Loury, Glenn. "How to Mend Affirmative Action." *Public Interest* (March 22 1997).

Malamud, Deborah. "Affirmative Action, Diversity, and the Black Middle Class." *University of Colorado Law Review* 68 (1997): 939–99.

——. "Assessing Class-Based Affirmative Action." *Journal of Legal Education* 47 (1997): 452–71.

Massey, Douglas, and Nancy Denton. *American Apartheid.* Cambridge, MA: Harvard University Press, 1993.

McGary, Jr., Howard. "Justice and Reparations." *Philosophical Forum* 9 (1977–78): 250–63.

Merritt, Deborah Jones. "The Future of Bakke: Will Social Science Matter?" *Ohio State Law Journal* 59 (1998): 1054–67.

Michaels, Walter Benn. *The Trouble with Diversity.* New York: Metropolitan Books, 2006.

Morris, Christopher. "Existential Limits to the Rectification of Past Wrongs." *American Philosophical Quarterly* 21 (1984): 175–82.

Moskos, Charles. "Success Story: Blacks in the Military." *Atlantic Monthly* (May 1986), http://www.theatlantic.com/politics/defense/moskos.htm.

Mosley, Albert, and Nicholas Capaldi. *Affirmative Action: Social Justice or Unfair Preference.* Lanham, MD: Rowman and Littlefield, 1996.

Moor, Jamillah. *Race and College Admissions.* Jefferson, NC: McFarland, 2005.

Murphy, Evelyn, with E. J. Graff. *Getting Even.* New York: Simon & Shuster, 2005.

Murray, Charles. "Affirmative Racism." In *Morality in Practice,* edited by James P. Sterba, 251–57, 6th ed. Belmont, CA: Wadsworth, 2000.

Muwakkil, Salim. "Have We Put Racism Behind Us? Don't Kid Yourselves." *Wall Street Journal,* September 29, 2003.

Navetta, Jean-Marie. "Gains in Learning, Gaps in Earning." *AAUW Outlook* (Spring 2005).

Neckerman, Kathryn M., and Joleen Kirschenman. "Hiring Strategies, Racial Bias and Inner-City Workers." *Social Problems* 38 (1991): 433, 437–41.

Needham, Amie. "Leveling the Playing Field—Affirmative Action in the European Union." *New York Law School Journal of International and Comparative Law* 19 (2000): 479–97.

Newton, Lisa. "Reverse Discrimination as Unjustified." *Ethics* 83 (1973): 308–12.

Nickel, James. "Should Reparations Be to Individuals or Groups?" *Analysis* (1974): 154–60.

Orfield, Gary. "The Resegregation of Our Nation's School." *Civil Rights Journal* (Fall 1999): 8–13.

Orfield, Gary, and John Yun. "Resegregation in American Schools." *The Civil Rights Project,* Harvard University, 1999, http://www.civilrightsproject.ucla.edu/research/deseg/reseg_schools99.php.

Paul, Ellen Frankel. "Set-Asides, Reparations, and Compensatory Justice." In *Compensatory Justice,* edited by John Chapman, 97–142. New York: New York University Press, 1991.

Pell, Terence. "Racial Preferences and Formal Equality." *Journal of Social Philosophy* 34 (2003): 309–25.

——. "The Nature of Claims about Race and the Debate over Racial Preferences." *International Journal of Applied Philosophy* (2004): 13–27.

Pojman, Louis. "The Case against Affirmative Action." In *Morality in Practice,* edited by James P. Sterba, 233–45. 6th. ed. Belmont, CA: Wadsworth, 2000.

——. "Straw Man or Straw Theory: A Reply to Mosley." *International Journal of Applied Philosophy* (1998): 169–80.

Post, Robert, and Michael Rogin, eds. *Race and Representation: Affirmative Action.* New York: Zone Books, 1998.

Purdy, Laura. "In Defense of Hiring Apparently Less Qualified Women." *Journal of Social Philosophy* 15 (1984): 26–33.

Robert, Albert. *Helping Battered Women.* New York: Oxford University Press, 1996.

Rosen, Jeffery. "Is Affirmative Action Doomed?" *New Republic,* October 17, 1994.

Rosenfeld, Michael. *Affirmative Action and Justice.* New Haven: Yale University Press, 1991.

Sander, Richard. "A Systemic Analysis of Affirmative Action at American Law Schools." *Stanford Law Review* 57 (2004): 367.

——. "A Reply to Critics." *Stanford Law Review* 57 (2005): 1963.

Schmidt, Peter. *Color and Money.* New York: Palgrave Macmillan, 2007.

Schnapper, Eric. "Affirmative Action and the Legislative History of the Fourteenth Amendment." *Virginia Law Review* 71 (1985): 753–98.

Sher, George. *Approximate Justice.* Lanham, MD: Rowman and Littlefield, 1997.

Siegel, Reva. "The Racial Rhetorics of Colorblind Constitutionalism: The Case of Hopwood v. Texas." In *Race and Representation: Affirmative Action,* edited by Robert Post and Michael Rogin, 29–72. New York: Zone Books, 1998.

Simon, Robert. "Affirmative Action and Faculty Appointments." In *Affirmative Action and the University,* edited by Steven Cahn, 93–121. Philadelphia: Temple University Press, 1993.

Skrentny, John. *The Ironies of Affirmative Action.* Chicago: University of Chicago, 1996.

Sowell, Thomas. *Affirmative Action Reconsidered.* Washington, DC: American Enterprise Institute for Public Policy Research, 1975.

———. *Civil Rights: Rhetoric or Reality?* New York: William Morrow, 1984.

———. *Preferential Policies: An International Perspective.* New York: William Morrow, 1990.

———. *Race and Culture.* New York: Basic Books, 1994.

Steele, Claude. "The Compelling Need for Diversity in Higher Education." *Gratz v. Bollinger,* no. 97-75231 (E.D. Mich.) (2000).

Steele, Claude, and Joshua Aronson. "Stereotype Threat and the Intellectual Text Performance of African Americans." *Journal of Personality and Social Psychology* 69 (1995): 797–811.

Steinberg, Stephen. *Turning Back: The Retreat from Racial Justice in American Thought and Policy.* Boston: Beacon Press, 1995.

Sterba, James P. *Justice for Here and Now.* Cambridge, MA: Cambridge University Press, 1998.

———. *Three Challenges to Ethics.* New York: Oxford University Press, 2001.

Sturm, Susan, and Lani Guinier. "The Future of Affirmative Action: Reclaiming the Innovative Ideal." *California Law Review* 84 (1996).

Sunstein, Cass. "Why Markets Don't Stop Discrimination." In *Free Markets and Social Justice,* 151–66. Oxford: Oxford University Press, 1997.

Taylor, Bron. *Affirmative Action at Work: Law, Politics, and Ethics.* Pittsburgh: University of Pittsburgh Press, 1991.

Taylor, Paul. "Reserve Discrimination and Compensatory Justice." *Analysis* 33 (1973): 177–82.

Tummala, Krishua. "Policy of Preference: Lessons from India, the United States and South Africa." *Public Administration Review* 59 (1999): 495–508.

Wasserstrom, Richard. "Racism, Sexism and Preferential Treatment." *UCLA Law Review* 24 (1977): 581.

Watkins, Steve. *The Black O: Racism and Redemption in an American Corporate Empire.* Athens: University of Georgia Press, 1997.

Weiss, Robert J. *We Want Jobs.* New York: Garland, 1997.

Weisskoff, Thomas. "Consequences of Affirmative Action in U.S. Higher Education: A Review of Recent Empirical Studies." *Economic and Political Weekly,* December 22, 2001.

Woo, Deborah. *Glass Ceilings and Asian Americans.* Lanham, MD: Rowman and Littlefield, 2000.

Court Cases and Legal Documents

The Fourteenth Amendment to the U.S. Constitution, 1868

The Civil Rights Act of 1964

Contractors Association of Eastern Pennsylvania v. the Secretary of Labor 442 F.2d 159 (1971)

Griggs v. Duke Power, Co. (1971)

EEOC v. AT&T, 365 F. Supp. 1105 (1973)

DeFunis v. Odegaard 416 U.S 312 (1974)

Marks v. United States (1977)

Regents of the University of California v. Bakke 438 U.S. 265 (1978)

United Steelworkers of America v. Weber 443 U.S. 193 (1979)

Fullilove v. Klutznick 448 U.S. 448 (1980)

Geier v. Alexander, Sixth Circuit 593 F. Supp. 1263 (1986)

Johnson v. Transportation Agency of Santa Clara County 480 U.S. 616 (1986)

Local 28 v. EEOC 478 U.S. 421 (1986)

Wygant v. Jackson Board of Education 476 U.S. 267 (1986)

City of Richmond v. J.A. Croson Co. 488 U.S. 469 (1989)

Wards Cove v. Antonio (1989)

Civil Rights Act of 1991

Podberesky v. Kirwan, District Court Court of Appeals 838 F. Supp. 1075 (1993)

Adarand Constructors v. Pena 516 U.S. 200 (1995)

Hopwood v. Texas, Fifth Circuit 518 U.S. 1033 (1995)

Proposition 209 (1996)

Marschall v. Land Nordrein-Westfalen CaseC-409/95 (1997)

Gratz v. Bollinger, District Court 122 F. Supp. 2nd 874 (2000)

Grutter v. Bollinger, District Court 137 F. Supp. 2nd (2001)

Gratz v. Bollinger 539 U.S. (2003)

Grutter v. Bollinger, 539 U.S. (2003)

Proposition 2 (2006)

Operation King's Dream v. Ward Connerly, 2006 U.S. Dist. Lexis 61323 (2006)

Parents Involved in Community v. Seattle School District and *Crystal Meredith v. Jefferson Country Board of Education* 426 F. 3d 1162 (2007)

Index